# I AM A PALESTINIAN CHRISTIAN

# I AM A PALESTINIAN CHRISTIAN

## Mitri Raheb

TRANSLATED BY Ruth C. L. Gritsch

WITH A FOREWORD BY
Rosemary Radford Ruether

FORTRESS PRESS
MINNEAPOLIS

I Am a Palestinian Christian

Biblical quotations are from the *New Revised Standard Version of the Bible,* copyright © 1989 by the Division of Christian Education of the National Council of Churches of Christ in the USA and are used by permission.

Cover photo: Bethlehem. Photograph provided by Photoreporters Inc., Deutsche Presse, Frankfurt.
Cover design: Peggy Lauritsen Design Group
Interior design: Peregrine Graphics Services

Library of Congress Cataloging-in-Publication data
Raheb, Mitri.
    I am a Palestinian Christian : Mitri Raheb ; translated by Ruth C. L. Gritsch ; with a foreword by Rosemary Radford Ruether.
      p.   cm.
    Includes bibliographical references (p.   ).
    ISBN 0-8006-2663-X (alk. paper)
    1. Palestine in Christianity. 2. Christianity—Palestine. 3. Palestine in the Bible. 4. Israel (Christian theology) 5. Palestine—Church history—20th century. 6 Palestine—Politics and government—1948– 7. Raheb, Mitri. I. Title.
BT93.8.R34   1995
275.694—dc20                            95-5483
                                            CIP

Manufactured in the U.S.A.                            AF 1-2663
                                4     5     6     7     8     9    10

# CONTENTS

TO THE ONE WHOSE LOVE,
ENCOURAGEMENT, AND SUPPORT
MADE THIS WORK POSSIBLE:
MY WIFE, NAJWA

# FOREWORD

MITRI RAHEB is a Palestinian Arab Lutheran Christian pastor who ministers in his hometown of Bethlehem. For many American Christians this combination of identities is incomprehensible. They assume that Palestinian Arabs are Muslims, not Christians, much less Lutherans. Their first question is likely to be, "When did you become a Christian?" assuming him to be a recent convert from Islam. Raheb writes as a cultural mediator to the Western Christian world and as a local theologian for the Palestinian Christian community.

Raheb wishes Western Christians to understand the Palestinian Christians' reality, of which they have been deeply ignorant and whom they have injured and betrayed in that ignorance. He also grapples with how Palestinian Christians can develop a local theology that can be both truthful and helpful in mediating the conflicts between Israel and Palestine and among Christianity, Judaism, and Islam. Both are conflicts in which religion, politics, and collective identity intertwine.

To the question, "When did you become a Christian?" Raheb, like all Palestinian Christians, would reply something like, "Sometime in the first to third centuries." Palestinian Christians, including those who today may be Lutherans, are not recent converts to Christianity from Islam but the remnant of the ancient Palestinian Christian community who were the religious majority in Palestine by the fourth century. In that time Bethlehem was entirely Christian. Palestinian Christians in Palestine today are survivors who remained steadfast in their faith and their land under thirteen centuries of Islamic rule and almost fifty years of Israeli rule.

Unlike Western Christians, Palestinian Christians have almost no experience being the ruling political group. Even in the Byzantine period, they often belonged to Christian groups not favored by the emperor. In the Islamic period that began in the seventh century, they became a dwindling minority, as many of their brethren became Muslims. Today their numbers in the Holy Land are diminishing under Israeli pressure to emigrate, to the point where they worry that the ancient Christian churches will be empty of local Christians.

Although Palestinian Christians have lived most of their history as a minority and today as a minority within an occupied and subjugated people, they have also been cultural mediators between majority peoples and cultures. In the Islamic centuries they mediated Greek culture to the Arabs. Today they mediate between the Islamic Arab world and the Christian West. Raheb's book is itself an expression of this work of mediation.

Palestinian Christians are themselves the heirs of the many historic Christian heritages, from the schisms of the fifth century to the divisions of the Reformation, all of which have affected the Palestinian Christian community, dividing and subdividing it. Raheb's ancestors were Greek Orthodox until the early twentieth century. They became Lutheran when his orphaned grandfather was taken to a German Lutheran school to be raised. To knit together their local Christian community, Palestinian Christians must be the most inclusive of ecumenists, including the Middle East Council of Churches, Old Catholics and Orthodox Catholics (Uniate and Roman), and all varieties of Protestants.

Palestinian Christians also reach beyond Christianity to envision an ecumenical kinship of the three Abrahamic faiths, Judaism, Christianity and Islam. As a Bethlehemite, Raheb grew up thinking of both David and Jesus as his local kin, as well as his religious ancestors. As a Palestinian he is an integral part of the Palestinian Arab community, the majority of which are Muslims. One of Mohammed's first wives was a Christian, and the Qur'an cannot be understood without recognizing its overlapping relationship with both Christianity and Judaism.

Christians were both tolerated by Islam as "people of the book" and marginalized as second-class groups within the Islamic superstate. This impelled Christians in the Islamic world to become a "modernizing" cultural elite, seeking to separate religion and state to create secular Arab nation-states where they could enjoy equal citizenship. But secular nationalism has not fulfilled its promise of equality and justice, and so Arab Christians are faced with Islamic fundamentalist movements that would reestablish Islamic states where *shari'a* (Islamic law) would reign and

Arab Christians, as well as other religious minorities, would be marginalized and perhaps even persecuted.

If Palestinian Christians stand in danger of being betrayed by their Muslim brothers, they also have been betrayed by their Western Christian co-religionists. Wishing to repent of their sins of anti-Semitism against Jews, which resulted in the Holocaust, Western Christians mythologize the state of Israel as a "sign of redemption" and a fulfillment of God's promise to the Jews, ignoring the injustice to the Palestinians. For the Palestinians and the Arab world generally, Zionists have been Western colonists who brought with them religious myths of election and divine promise of the land to displace the local inhabitants from their historic homeland.

For Palestinians the state of Israel has not meant redemption but catastrophe, which has led to progressive land confiscation, expulsion, and daily violation of their human rights. Western Christian collaboration with this violence to assuage their consciences toward Jews has made Palestinians pay the price of Western "repentance." Since this violence and oppression are justified by both Jews and Western Christians in the name of the Bible, this situation has thrown Palestinian Christians into a conflictive relation with their own Scripture. How can Palestinian Christians today read biblical ideas—concepts such as Israel as God's elect people, the promised land, and the Exodus from Egypt to the promised land—without seeing themselves as victims of God's redemptive actions on behalf of others against themselves?

Palestinian Christians today stand between a secular nationalism that has proven inadequate to the demands of justice and reconciliation between peoples, and Muslim and Jewish Zionist fundamentalisms that offer them no hope but only the threat of further oppression as a minority religious community in dominant Jewish or Islamic states. There is no Christian fundamentalism into which they can retreat to find a place for themselves in this conflict of religion and state. For many the solution has been immigration to the West.

If Palestinian Christians are to remain steadfast in their own land and also find in their religious tradition the revelatory and redemptive insights to mediate these conflicts, they must develop a local Palestinian theology, a reading of the Bible from their context, which calls all parties—Palestinians and Israelis, Jews, Christians, and Muslims—into just and peaceful relations with each other, under the one God in whom they all profess to believe. The second half of Raheb's book explores the exegetical method for such a liberative and reconciling theology from the Palestinian Christian context.

Key to this exegesis is the basic Christian insight that the God revealed in the Bible, the God who is revealed in Jesus Christ, is not a God of one nation or one people only, but a God of all nations, who calls all people to justice and peace toward one another. As in the book of Jonah, God is as much the God of the Ninevites as the God of Israel and calls God's prophets to transcend their ethnic chauvinism and become instruments of redemption to those whom they have regarded as their enemies. Doctrines, such as exodus, election, and promise of the land, must be read in the context of this inclusive relation to God and inclusive call to justice and peace, and not as claims to dominance of one group against another.

Mitri Raheb ends his book with a line from Martin Luther King, Jr.: "I have a dream." Raheb's dream is that of two peoples and three religions all sharing the one land of Palestine in justice and peace. He calls Western Christians to be helpers, rather than hinderers, in realizing that dream.

—ROSEMARY RADFORD RUETHER

# ACKNOWLEDGMENTS

THIS BOOK has its origin in a number of lectures and sermons delivered at local and international conferences during the last several years. Many changes in the political situation of the Middle East have taken place during this time. In spite of these changes, the issues dealt with in this book remain of great importance to the local Palestinians as well as to the worldwide Christian community.

I would like to acknowledge with gratitude the support of many friends and colleagues whose efforts have made the publishing of this book possible: Professor Clifford Green of Hartford Seminary, for making the initial contact with Fortress Press; Dr. Marshall Johnson, Publishing Director of Fortress Press, for supporting the project and editing the translation; Ruth Gritsch for translating the manuscript from German to English; and Dr. Roger Williamson, for reviewing the manuscript and offering many valuable suggestions.

# PART 1
# On Being a Palestinian Christian

# CHAPTER 1

# MY IDENTITY AS A CHRISTIAN PALESTINIAN

IS THERE such a thing as a Christian Palestinian or Palestinian Christian? Can a Christian understand himself or herself to be a Palestinian? Can a Palestinian be simultaneously a Christian? How? Who are these Christian Palestinians? Where do they come from? What do they think? How do they define themselves? What are their distinctive characteristics and their problems? What determines their identity? These are questions I shall try to answer. I hope to be able to make the identity of many Christian Palestinians clear by describing how I see myself as a Christian Palestinian.

I was born in Bethlehem on June 26, 1962, into a family that took root in this city a very long time ago. The Raheb family has lived in and around Bethlehem for many centuries. This small and insignificant city has, in the course of history, attained a particular worldwide renown. It was here that in 1000 B.C.E. David was born, out of the tribe of Jesse, later to become the anointed king of Israel. But Bethlehem's particular claim to historical fame is that it was the birthplace of Jesus the Christ. It was through him that "Bethlehem of Ephrathah, who are one of the little clans" (Micah 5:2) became "by no means least among the rulers of Judah" (Matt 2:6).

My identity was stamped by the fact that I was born in this particular place. I feel I have something like a special relationship to David and to Christ—a relationship developed not only by way of the Bible, not only through faith, but also by way of the land. I share my city and my land with David and with Jesus. My self-understanding as a Christian Palestinian has a territorial dimension. I feel that I am living in a continuity of locale with these biblical figures, sharing the same landscape, culture, and environment with them. One need not make a pilgrimage, since one is already at the source itself, at the point of origin. That is why this city of Bethlehem and this land of Palestine are enormously important to me. They do not merely help me live, they are a part of my identity.

A kind of symbiosis exists between the land of Palestine and Christian Palestinians. Each has influenced and imprinted the other deeply. The fact that God chose this place to become human and that here Christ suffered, was crucified, and rose again has transformed the whole history of Palestine and has given it its own peculiar demographic, economic, and topographical character. Many Christians throughout the centuries have been attracted to this land and have moved here as a result.

Although Palestine was once a Christian land, with the passage of time more and more Christians were assimilated, and their number decreased. The Christian Palestinians of today are nothing else than the Christian remnant that has remained steadfast despite all the persecutions in Palestine. These Christians live where the most important events of revelation took place. About 30,000 live in and around Bethlehem, the city of the Incarnation; about 20,000 live in and around Jerusalem, the city of the cross and Resurrection; and approximately 100,000 Christian Palestinians live in and around Nazareth, the city of the Annunciation. About 320,000 other Christian Palestinians live in the diaspora.

Christianity disappeared from many cities in the course of the centuries but survived in the holy sites. In times of war, both Christians and Muslims sought refuge in the great and historically significant churches. I can still remember the Six Day War in 1967: shortly after war broke out and Israel started shelling Bethlehem, my mother carried me to the Church of the Nativity, where we and many other Christian families from Bethlehem found refuge. We all lived together in the rooms of the church for the duration of the war. This is where we felt safe and secure despite the bombardments.

At the same time, Christians have always felt responsible for protecting and defending these churches and sites, which made for mutual support. The fate of the Christians is thus bound up with the fate of their holy sites. The fact that Christian Palestinians have refused to abandon these holy sites despite massive pressure demonstrates that the holy sites are almost meaningless to them if there is not a Christian community living and worshiping there. The stones of the church need the living stones, but we living stones need a space and a locality in which to live and to celebrate. That is why both the land of Palestine and the holy sites are part of the Palestinian Christian identity.

Born in Bethlehem, I was given the name of my grandfather Mitri. My full name is Mitri Bishara Mitri Konstantin al-Raheb. One can derive many things from this name. The name of my great-grandfather refers to the Emperor Constantine who reigned 306–337 and reunited the Roman Empire. He was the first emperor to convert to Christianity, and the Christian church was consciously fostered by the state during his time. The emperor's policy left visible traces in Bethlehem as well, for Emperor Constantine's mother Helena visited Bethlehem on her journey to Palestine in 324. In response to her plea, the emperor had a basilica built two years later over the grotto in which, according to tradition, Christ had been born.[1] This made Bethlehem one of the first and most important Christian pilgrimage sites in Palestine.

By the fourth century at the latest, Bethlehem was inhabited exclusively by Christians. Some of these Christians were descended from Jews who had believed in Jesus as the Messiah and who had chosen to stay in Bethlehem.[2] But Bethlehem proved to be a powerful attraction for Christians in the whole world. After the conquest of Rome by the Western Goths, many Christians sought refuge in Bethlehem. The noted church father Jerome retired to Bethlehem from Rome in 386 to spend the last 34 years of his life there as a monk and scholar. It was here in Bethlehem that he completed the Latin translation of the Bible known as the Vulgate.

The position of Christians in the Roman Empire changed drastically after Constantine's conversion. As a result of the so-called Edict of Milan (313), Christians experienced a transformation in their social status and power. They were no longer the persecuted minority. They were tolerated, and a little later they even attained positions of power.

Many Christians considered this assumption of power to be alien to true Christianity. They felt that the church had become secularized, that nothing much remained of the exemplary faith of the martyrs, and that this faith had instead been compromised and watered down. These Christians could not identify with a kind of Christianity contradicting that of the first two centuries and appearing to them as an aberration. Consequently, many of them withdrew into the wilderness to become monks. More than 130 monastic communities were established in the wilderness in the immediate vicinity of Bethlehem between the fourth and the sixth centuries. The wilderness began to bloom, not with flowers but with monasteries.[3] These monasteries played a considerable role in Christian piety, Palestinian theology, and Middle Eastern church politics of the following centuries. Monasticism played a role in the history of my own family too, for my family name indicates that one of my ancestors was a monk for a time. The name *Raheb* is Arabic for "monk."

My grandfather, whose name I also bear, was named Mitri. The name Mitri, originally the name of a Greek deity, is the Arabic form of the name of Saint Demetrius, a name prevalent in the Greek and Russian Orthodox churches. Thus I bear a Greek Orthodox name even though I am myself an Evangelical Lutheran pastor.

This coexistence of various churches is typical of Christianity in Palestine. Unlike the European situation, there never existed in Palestine a monopolistic church claiming that there could be no salvation outside itself. Moreover, Christianity here has from the very beginning been pluralistic, manifest in many different forms.

From a Eurocentric perspective, the first church schism seems to have occurred through Martin Luther in the Middle Ages. But if one knows the history of Eastern Christianity, one knows that the first church schism occurred as early as the fifth or sixth century c.e. A number of different churches were already being created amid the confusion of political developments and dogmatic arguments of that time. The Greek Orthodox Church is an outgrowth of the church of the old Byzantine Empire. A number of so-called Eastern churches grew along with it, among them the Assyrian Church of the East, the Coptic Orthodox Church, the Syrian Orthodox (Jacobite) Church, and the Armenian Orthodox (Gregorian) Church.[4]

The first contact between these Eastern churches and the Roman Catholic Church in the West did not take place until the Middle Ages, when new schisms occurred as a result of their contact. In the fifteenth century, in particular, a variety of churches were established in union with Rome. These churches maintained the Eastern rite in their tradition and liturgy but recognized the primacy of the pope.[5] In the nineteenth century, missionary efforts created new schisms, giving rise to the Roman Catholic,[6] Lutheran,[7] Anglican, and Presbyterian churches.[8]

This diversity of confessions is unique. It is simultaneously a blessing and a curse, for therein lies the strength but also the weakness in the Middle Eastern churches. Thus ecumenism is a dire necessity. It is necessary so as to give each church a share "in the richness of tradition and spiritual experience of the others."[9] It is also necessary in order to render the church's testimony to the world credible (especially since we are here dealing with the non-Christian world). In order to come closer to these goals, all Orthodox, Eastern, and Protestant churches in the Middle

East formed the Middle East Council of Churches (MECC) in 1974.[10] The churches in the Catholic tradition joined in 1989, so that all the churches of the region (with the exception of the Assyrian Church of the East) are now represented in the MECC.

This diversity also explains why I bear a Greek Orthodox name even though I am an Evangelical Lutheran pastor. The great majority of Christians in Palestine belonged to the Greek Orthodox Church until the beginning of the last century. So too did my great-grandfather Constantine. He died young, leaving a small son, Mitri. Some relatives took the orphaned boy and brought him to Father Schneller[11] in Jerusalem. Father Johann Ludwig Schneller, a true Swabian from Southern Germany who had come to Jerusalem as a Chrischona brother in 1854, had founded the Syrian Orphanage in 1860. His purpose had been to give orphans from Greater Syria (encompassing today's Syria, Lebanon, Jordan, and Palestine) a home, provide a school for them, and enable them to learn a trade. All of this was related to Christian education and permeated by a Christian atmosphere, in the hope that the orphans would later prove to be true Christians and form a network of Christian cells throughout Palestine.

My orphaned grandfather Mitri was accepted into this Syrian Orphanage in 1868. That is where he found a home after the death of his parents; that is where he went to school and learned a trade; and that is where my Greek Orthodox grandfather was confronted with the Protestant faith. He decided to have Father Schneller confirm him a few years later, and from then on my grandfather could never shake off this Protestant faith.

My grandfather returned to his hometown of Bethlehem after graduating from the Schneller School and tried to be a faithful member of his Greek Orthodox Church despite his confirmation in the Protestant faith. But he missed the Protestant sermons, pastoral care, and instruction. As a matter of fact, conditions in the Greek Orthodox Church had degenerated greatly (especially after the start of Ottoman rule over Palestine at the beginning of the sixteenth century). The non-native (Greek) leadership of this church was more interested in the holy sites than in the people, while the Arab priests were uneducated and powerless. Lay members despaired and suffered greatly under these conditions. After a confrontation with the Greek Orthodox hierarchy, my grandfather was compelled to join the Protestant congregation[12] in Bethlehem, which had been founded in 1854.

With the help of the Lutheran World Council, all the Arab-Palestinian congregations that had grown out of the German Evangelical missions formed the Evangelical Lutheran Church in Jordan[13] in 1959. That is why I am a third-generation Evangelical Lutheran Christian of Greek Orthodox extraction.

My grandfather named his third son, my father, Bischara, the Arabic designation for the Greek *Evangelion,* which means gospel, joyful tidings, or good news. The Arabic *bischara* is also the name of a Christian feast, namely, the feast of the angel's annunciation of Jesus' birth to Mary. But why do Christians bear Arabic names? What does Arabia have to do with Christianity? Someone could very well ask this question in amazement, especially since the West equates "Arab" with "Muslim." This is certainly a misapprehension of both Middle Eastern history and Christianity, for Arab Christians are not a new invention, nor a Western product, nor goods imported into the Middle East. Arab Christians date back to the first century. The Evangelist Luke reports in Acts 2:11 that Arabs were present at the first feast of Pentecost. Thus Arab Christians were among the very first Christians. Consequently it is not surprising that the Apostle Paul retired into Arabia immediately after his conversion (Gal 1:17). This area, southeast of Damascus, was the probable home of those Arabs who had been in Jerusalem at Pentecost, rather than a pagan territory. If this is in fact true, then Arab Christians played a decisive role in shaping Paul's theology.

Christian mission among the Arab tribes in both Mesopotamia and the Arabian peninsula in the first six centuries was very successful, although no independent Arabian church was established there. Instead, these Arab Christians remained divided among a variety of Eastern churches as well as among diverse political realms.[14]

When Mohammed appeared as a prophet in Mecca at the beginning of the seventh century, various forms of Christianity were playing a considerable role in that area.[15] Hermitages could be found everywhere, parts of Holy Scripture were already available in Arabic, and there were already several Christian preachers in the Arabian centers of trade. Even some of Mohammed's relatives were Christians, including his first wife's cousin Khadija. Khadija had entrusted her commercial affairs to her husband, Mohammed, who became acquainted with Christian monks on his sales trips. He heard Christian preachers deliver sermons that impressed him greatly. It is therefore not surprising that the Qur'an substantially overlaps the Old and New Testaments in several places. As a result, Christians in the Arabian peninsula considered Islam to be not so much a "new religion, but rather a new direction in Christian faith."[16] The prophet Mohammed found it possible to unify the feuding Arab tribes through this new religion as well as through the Arabic language that was related to it. These Arab tribes, unified under Islam, soon became the most important political, military, and economic power of the world at that time.

Palestine was conquered in 637 under the leadership of the Caliph Omar-al-Khattab, the second successor to Mohammed. This marks the start of the "Arabization" of Palestine and the Near East. When Omar came to Bethlehem shortly afterward, he visited the Church of the Nativity. At the hour of prayer he retired into the right wing of the church and prayed there.[17] This place was a holy site also to him as a Muslim, for his Qur'an mentions the birth of Jesus. Omar gave the Greek Orthodox patriarch of Jerusalem written assurance that he would spare Christian churches and allow Christians free access to them.[18]

A few Christian Arab tribes from the Arabian peninsula arrived in Palestine at almost the same time as the caliph. Two of them settled in Bethlehem, and their descendants still live in two of the eight city districts.[19] Some Muslims came to Bethlehem with the caliph and settled there, but they remained a minority in the ensuing centuries; by the middle of this century there were Muslims living in only one district of Bethlehem. Today, however, Muslims constitute about 60 percent of the population.

This pluralistic, multireligious, and multicultural society has always been typical of Arab Christianity's environment. Almost never in history was Christianity the sole ruling component. People who thought differently and believed differently from each other have always been a part of its world. Islam has been the most significant component in the world of Arab Christianity for almost 1400 years. Arab Christians and Muslims share the same Arabic culture, history, and language; their fate is intertwined and inseparable. Likewise, Arab Christians are an inseparable part of the world of Islam. Dialogue with Muslims is a necessary and important aspect of Arab Christians' life and survival. Arab Christians are a minority in the Islamic world. There are about 14 million Christians in a world of more than 200 million Muslims.[20] This, too, is typical of the history of Arab Christians. They have hardly ever been the people with power, which is what prevented them from being persecutors and exploiters. But this also meant that they were never quite spared suffering.

Arab Christians are a minority, but only a quantitative, not a qualitative minority. They have never been a marginalized, self-obsessed group. They achieved great things at the most important junctures of history and enriched the world community of both East and West. In the seventh and eighth centuries, it was Syrian Christians who translated the Greek philosophical tradition into Arabic and thus made it available to the Islamic world.[21] And in the Middle Ages, it was Arab Christians who made the philosophical, medical, and scientific inheritance of Arabia available to Europe.[22] Furthermore, it was Arab Christians who shook the Arab world out of its deep medieval sleep in the nineteenth century, promoted the renaissance of Arab culture and language, and introduced modern ideas and values to the Arab world.[23]

That, by the way, is one of the characteristics of Arab Christians. Whereas a large number of Western Christians tend to be more or less conservative, the majority of Arab Christians are aligned on the side of progress. This has been determined by history: modern Western Christianity has been shaped by its discussion with the Enlightenment. Western churches tended to assume a defensive, conservative, and self-engrossed stance in reaction to the emerging Enlightenment. Arab Christians, on the other hand—on the basis of their position as a minority in an Islamic world—were more likely to align themselves with progress and to be receptive to innovations.

Another important factor must be mentioned in this regard. Just as Arab Christians are an inseparable part of the Arab Islamic world, so are they an inseparable part of the Christian world. They belong to both the Arab nation and the universal church. Belonging to two worlds has, for centuries, constituted a great challenge not easy to resolve. Sometimes it seemed as though Arab Christians fell between two chairs. They were often misunderstood and even betrayed by both sides.

Arab Christians were sometimes made forcefully aware that their Western co-religionists cultivated a Christianity strange to them. Arab Christian existence was strongly linked to the sign of the cross from the very beginning. To them, the cross was the reality of a suffering church rather than the inheritance of a triumphant church. Western churches, on the other hand, related the sign of the cross to power, vested interests, and expansion. To some extent, the slogan became "crusade" rather than "follow in the way of the cross." Moreover, Arab Christians still suffer today as a result of the appearance in the nineteenth century of so-called Christian nations in the West, which, in the role of imperialists, carved up their land, plundered their resources, and oppressed them. Arab Christians hoped repeatedly that these Western, allegedly Christian nations would let justice prevail, but the predominant pattern was one of trade in weapons, divisive favoritism, and new forms of injustice. The German emperor's political support of the Ottoman regime at the beginning of the twentieth century, England's help in the creation of a Jewish homeland in Palestine, and the United States' subsidies to Israel are only a few examples.

It is precisely because Arab Christians have often suffered the consequences of these policies that a dialogue with their brothers and sisters in the West is an important task for both sides. But Arab Christians were also able to profit very often from this double belonging. They were able to obtain help from their brothers and sisters in the West and, at the same time, arouse understanding for the Arab world. They often functioned as transcenders of borders and as bridge builders.

One final fact must be mentioned: the Bible already referred to Bethlehem, my city, as "Ephrathah," meaning "fruitful."[24] From the very beginning, therefore, Bethlehem has been neither infertile nor uncultivated. On the contrary, Bethlehem's soil is fruitful for both grain and fruit. That is why the city is known as "house of bread" (*Beit lechem*) in Hebrew and as "house of meat" in Arabic.[25] Therefore it is not surprising that, in the course of history, Bethlehem was the site of a variety of fertility cults. What applies to Bethlehem applies equally to all of Palestine, which is part of the fertile crescent. For the nomadic Israelites, Palestine was a land where "milk and honey flow," a land so valuable that it became the object of a promise (a promise, by the way, that always depended on God, just as the land's fertility depended on rain).

Palestine is also a land "blessed" by its geographical location, for:

> Palestine has served as a bridge in two ways since early in history: it is the only land bridge between Africa and Asia on the one hand, and between the Mediterranean and the Red sea on the other, which means between the Atlantic and Indian oceans. . . . As an important crossroad of two international [trade] routes it became the focal point of cultural emissions such as the three monotheistic religions. But it also became the bone of contention among almost all the great powers, which could not avoid this narrow passage in their efforts at expansion.[26]

So if this land was blessed by God, it was also fought over and torn apart by human beings. During the course of history, blessing has repeatedly turned into curse. The great powers have attempted to acquire Palestine's riches for themselves, to exploit and suppress its people. These great powers wanted Palestine as the setting for their wars with each other where they could fight their decisive battles. The fertile plains of Palestine were transformed into battlefields. That is why it has been poverty rather than wealth, war instead of peace, and conflicts of interest rather than mutual cooperation that have prevailed in Palestine since time immemorial.

Five powers have ruled over Palestine in this century alone. At the beginning of this century, Palestine was part of the Ottoman Empire. After World War I it came under British Mandate. The Jordanians and Egyptians divided what was left, the West Bank and the Gaza Strip, after the creation of Israel in 1948. And Israel has been occupying the West Bank and the Gaza Strip, as well as East Jerusalem, since 1967. This land has suffered two world wars and no less than seven other regional wars in this century alone. This means that there has been a war in this country every ten years. When there was no war, there was no peace either—at best it was a truce. The various powers that have ruled Palestine in this century have exploited and oppressed the country in various forms and to various degrees. But all have had two things in common.

First, the people in power and the rulers were never people who came from Palestine. All were foreigners. The native population never had an opportunity to exercise political power. Palestine never experienced democracy, the rule of the people.

Second, the alien rulers were always interested in the land itself, in its resources and wealth. They hardly ever demonstrated serious interest in the indigenous Palestinian population. The land was always used and exploited in the interest of foreigners; the native population was always neglected and oppressed.

The Arab peoples, influenced by the European idea of national identity, started to oppose Ottoman rule as early as the end of the nineteenth century. A pan-Arabic movement was organized that had independence from the Ottomans as one of its goals. Zionism,[27] the Jewish national movement, was started in Europe at the same time.[28]

During World War I, the English used these two movements  to unite Arabs and Jews against the Ottomans. They promised Palestine as a reward to each.[29] But Palestine became a British Mandate and, for the first time in history, formed a separate entity. A state called Palestine was created, and the Palestinians living in it identified themselves increasingly with this state. Palestinian nationalism came into being.[30] There was a struggle over control of Palestine by Palestinian and Jewish nationalists during the time of the British Mandate. Yet whereas the Zionists were able to found a state of their own in 1948, the Palestinians remained without their own state.[31]

The state of Israel was established on the larger portion of Palestine, and demographic as well as topographical changes were made. Israel razed hundreds of Palestinian villages;[32] hundreds of thousands of Palestinians were driven out and made refugees;[33] the Palestinian diaspora was created. This has been deeply etched in the memory of Palestinians and is known to them as "the catastrophe."

Palestinians, whether in Palestine or in the diaspora, could not forget their country. They wanted to go on fighting for their homeland and for a state of their own. As a result, the Palestinian Liberation Organization was created in 1964. It soon became the representative of the Palestinian people.[34] The Israeli occupation of the West Bank merely strengthened the Palestinians' drive for independence. They realized that only a state of their own could guarantee their liberty, independence, and security. The Intifada is an expression of this Palestinian national determination.

To understand better Palestinian identity, it is important to know that Palestinians are not a racial subgroup:

> There is no specific ideal body type for the Palestinians that would distinguish them from the Europeans on the other side of the Mediterranean, be they Greeks, Italians, Southern-French or Spanish. Palestinian complexion ranges from olive tan to blue-white. . . . Palestinian hair ranges from black to auburn and, in certain areas, the district of Hebron for example, the Palestinians are blond and blue-eyed. In some families, the shape of the eyes and the jet-black soft hair betray Mongolian traces. . . . The highly diverse genetic pool that the different peoples who inhabited Palestine bequeathed us is reflected in the marked absence of a single Palestinian physical type.[35]

Instead, the Palestinian people have been shaped by three connections: to this land (mostly through birth), to the history and culture of this land, and to the suffering of this people:

Throughout ancient and modern history, the land of Palestine has been a veritable melting pot wherein diverse peoples and civilizations succeeded one another. As each civilization waned and lost its hold, its heritage was assimilated within the civilization that followed. Modern Palestinian cultural identity has taken shape under the influence of the various civilizations that reigned over the land of Palestine: Jebusites, Canaanites, Philistines, Hebrews, Amorites, Nabatians, Arameans, Persians, Greeks, Romans, and Arabs. The various Semitic and non-Semitic inhabitants of Palestine were first unified ideologically through Christianity. Between the seventh and ninth centuries, when the majority of the Palestinians converted to Islam and exchanged their various dialects for the Arabic language, the language of the Qur'an and that of the Moslem rulers, the seeds for a modern Palestinian cultural identity were sown.[36]

The land, due to its peculiar and tangled history as well as to the endless sufferings of its original population (especially their experience in this century of being denied self-determination, independence, and the right to live in their homeland), has endowed the Palestinian people with a special, unique, and deeply ingrained identity, which is shared by Christians and Moslems alike.

Economics and politics present a challenge to my faith in my identity as a Christian Palestinian. The piety I seek must be able to cope with these challenges. Christians in Palestine are forced to ask themselves what God's justice means to a people whose members suffer under systematic political, social, and economic injustice. What does "freedom in Christ" mean to people living under occupation and denied basic rights? What does the cross mean to a people constantly crucified and marked by suffering? And what does love for even an enemy mean to a people facing a heavily armed enemy?

# CHAPTER 2

# ON BEING A MINORITY

IT WAS NEAR the end of the 1970s. I had just finished my high school education and had decided to study theology. One of my friends came to see me and asked me whether I thought it made sense to study theology. He told me, "By the time you finish your studies, there will be no Christians left in Palestine. They will all have emigrated. The many churches of the Holy Land will have been transformed into museums, and you will be unemployed unless you work as a museum guide. But you don't need to study theology to do that."

I listened to his words with great sorrow, for I knew that he was not talking nonsense. More and more Palestinian Christians were leaving the Holy Land. They left their home and that of their ancestors to try their luck somewhere else; anywhere, where life is calmer, more peaceful, and more stable.

One of the greatest challenges confronting the Palestinian Christian today is emigration. Many have started to ask seriously whether there will be any native Christians left in the Holy Land in the near future, whether this country will become a kind of Christian Disneyland or theme park, and whether all that will remain here to visit and admire will be heaps of stones which have ceased being witnessing "living stones."

A quick look at the history of Palestinian Christian emigration in the last hundred years tends to confirm these fears. In the nineteenth century, about 15 percent of the population of Palestine was Christian. The corruption of Ottoman officials and the instability, tension, epidemics, and famine in the Ottoman Empire at the turn of the century forced Christians to consider emigration.[1]

Turks began to conscript Christians into the army after 1908, and emigration increased, with Christians from Bethlehem and the bordering town of Beit Jala being among the first to emigrate. Their destination was Central or South America. At present about 150,000 Christians from Bethlehem and Beit Jala are living in Central and South America, but only about 25,000 Christians are living in the Bethlehem area. Toward the end of the last century, Christians of Ramallah also started to emigrate to the United States to try their luck in that country of a thousand opportunities.

With the end of World War I came the end of the Ottoman Empire and the beginning of the British Mandate in Palestine. The massive Christian emigration abated, especially since many Christians found employment as officials in the various government departments. According to the English census of 1931, 80,000 Christians (10 percent of the Arab Palestinian population) were living in Palestine at that time. By the end of the 1940s, the figure had risen to about 135,000.[2]

This number would no doubt have been much higher if the English had not made it nearly impossible for Christian emigrants to return home after the war. But the British authorities imposed severe restrictions on the return of Christians who had left the country before the First World War, thus condemning them to a life in the diaspora.[3]

The Arab-Israel War of 1948 had catastrophic consequences for the 712,000 Palestinians who were driven out of their homes to become refugees. Among them were more than 50,000 Christians. Thus about 35 percent of all Christians living in Palestine lost all their possessions, their work, their lands and houses. About half of them fled to Lebanon. The other half settled in the West Bank and Jordan (7000 in East Jerusalem, 4500 in Bethlehem, 5500 in Ramallah, and 9000 in Amman and Madaba). The decline of Christian populations was rapid in the Christian cities of New Jerusalem (about 88 percent), Haifa (about 52 percent), Jaffa (about 73 percent), Ramallah (about 40 percent), and Lydda (about 70 percent). The number of Christians living in East Jerusalem and Bethlehem did increase, however.[4]

Between 1949 and 1967, the number of Christians increased in Israel, as well as in Jordan, including the West Bank. The number of Christians in Israel was about 30,000 in 1949, increasing to 60,000 by 1967. The number in Jordan rose from 93,000 in 1951 to 115,000 in 1964, including 46,000 Christians living on the West Bank at that time (according to the current definition of Occupied Territories, the number is 33,601 on the West Bank and 12,253 in East Jerusalem). Yet these numbers are misleading, since statistics indicate that the percentage rate in both states fell. In Israel it fell from 2.9 percent of the total population in 1949 to 2.2 percent in 1965; and in Jordan from 7.5 percent in 1951 to 6.6 percent in 1964.[5]

The main causes of the continuous though not massive Christian emigration from Israel and Jordan from the middle of the 1950s were the state of emergency imposed on the Arab population in Israel and Jordanian economic neglect of the West Bank. Most Christian emigrants went to the United States, Australia, and the Gulf states (the Gulf states were only accessible to the people of the West Bank). It should be pointed out that hundreds of thousands of Palestinians, including many Christians, have played an important role in developing the Gulf states.

The Six Day War of 1967, resulting in Israel's occupation of the West Bank, East Jerusalem, and the Gaza Strip, had enormous consequences for the Christians in these places. First Israel prohibited the return to their homes of all Palestinians who had by chance not been in the Occupied Territories during the war.[6] Among these were thousands of Christians. Again the Christian Palestinians were forced to lead a life in the diaspora.

But life was by no means easier for Christian Palestinians living in the Occupied Territories. These people suddenly became strangers in their own country. Life under the occupation compelled many Palestinian Christians to leave the country merely to get away from daily humiliation, tension, and servitude. Therefore, the absolute number of Christians living in Israel and Jordan may have risen since 1967, but the number of Christian Palestinians living in the Occupied Territories has been decreasing and now stands at 50,000. If one takes the birth rate into account, one can calculate that the number of Christians in the Occupied Territories should have doubled since 1967. Since this is not the case, it is safe to infer that half the Christians from the Occupied Territories have emigrated during the Israeli occupation. Emigration statistics between 1967 and 1986 indicate that approximately 166,000 Palestinians have left the West Bank and 103,000 have left the Gaza Strip. Thus a total of 269,000 Palestinians have left their homes and gone abroad.[7] If the instability caused by the occupation continues, Christian presence in the Holy Land will be seriously endangered. A 1990 study by the Al-Liqa Center, involving more than 550 Christian families in the Occupied Territories, provides alarming figures. According to the study, 22.3 percent of the families intended to emigrate in the next few years, and another 12.9 percent were considering that possibility.[8]

## The Basis and Background of Christian Emigration from Palestine

Anyone who studies Christian emigration from Palestine must keep two factors in view: the framework of Palestinian emigration in general and the special quality and nature of Christian emigration. Consequently, I shall first analyze it in its international framework, then in its Palestinian framework before moving on to its distinctive features as a widespread experience among Christians. I hope to find a new vision as a Palestinian on Palestinian soil when I draw my conclusions.

### 1. Emigration of Palestinian Christians in Global Perspective

Emigration is a global experience. There are emigrations from rural areas to the cities, from the south to the north, and from one country to another industrialized country. It is an ancient experience, beginning with the dawn of history. The history of humankind is nothing but a chain of successive emigrations. No country or continent has ever been spared, nor has a century passed without emigration.

Emigration is also a biblical experience. The fall is the story of Adam and Eve being forced to emigrate from Paradise. Salvation history starts with God's call to Abraham to leave his own country and move to one that God will show him. The Philistines and Israelites were migrant groups from Crete or Egypt. The person of faith is compared to a migrant who has no home on earth. The Bedouin background of the people in the Old Testament seems to have become a distinctive trait imbuing their followers with thoughts of wandering.

Emigration is a human experience. It is the result of human yearning for whatever is better and more elevated, the human search for what is superior and more sublime. It is the human quest to earn a living, attain psychological stability, and improve the quality of life. It is the right of every human being to emigrate; it belongs to freedom of choice.

Christian emigration from Palestine is therefore a part of this global experience, but this cannot account for it completely. I am attempting to analyze a special emigration, because the history of Palestine is special.

## 2. Christian Emigration within the Palestinian Framework

Palestine's recent history is connected to two significant movements. The first is the systematic and programmed expulsion of Palestinians from their land regardless of their religious beliefs, the result of a history of instability, wars, and occupations. The gravity of the problem lies in the fact that this drain has been continuing for the last hundred years.

The second is the programmed Jewish immigration and occupation of Palestinian lands in a kind of neocolonialism. The gravity of this problem lies in the fact that Jewish emigration to Palestine has been going on for more than 100 years.

Christians and Muslims alike have suffered and are still suffering from these two movements, as is clearly shown by the statistics. As a result of the 1948 war, for example, about 60,000 Christians and more than 600,000 Muslims emigrated or were forced to emigrate. That means that, of the emigrants or those forced to emigrate, Christians accounted for 10 percent. Now 55 percent (175,000) of Palestinian Christians reside in the diaspora, compared to the 145,000 still living in Palestine. The ratio is close to that of the total number of Palestinians living abroad (2,932,000—57.15 percent—compared to 2,201,400 living in Palestine).[9]

The experience of Christian emigration from Palestine, therefore, is not an exceptional one; it is an inseparable part of Palestinian emigration in general. There are nevertheless distinctive aspects of the Christian emigration from Palestine. Emigration poses an alarming threat to Palestinian Christian existence, particularly since Christians are still, more than others, threatened by emigration.

## 3. Special Aspects of Christian Emigration

### 1. SOCIAL FACTORS[10]

**a.** One important factor is demographics. The majority of Christians in Palestine lived and are still living in cities rather than in rural areas. Rural areas are habitually threatened by internal emigration to the cities, but cities are threatened by emigration to other countries.

**b.** Social class is important, since the majority of Christians live in the city and therefore belong to the middle class. Christian Arabs have in the past belonged to the class of artisans. Most of them were professionals and craftsmen, which is revealed clearly by their names (translated into English, they would be Smith, Carpenter, Taylor, and so on). In modern times, following the establishment of Christian schools, colleges, and universities in the cities, which were attended by more than 70 percent of the Christian population, the trend has been toward higher academic studies such as medicine, engineering, law, and so on.

It has been demonstrated that members of the middle class—professional specialists, academicians, white-collar workers—are more inclined to emigrate, because they are not bound to the land as are farmers and property owners. Moreover, their skills are in great demand, which results in tempting opportunities for them. The white-collar workers can use their expertise or art abroad too. They possess their mind and hands, and need not care for what must be sold in order to emigrate.

**c.** The language factor and continuity of contact with the West facilitate the emigration of the middle class. The Christian churches have been establishing and operating private schools that teach foreign languages as well as Arabic for the last hundred years. Christians have learned and mastered several Western languages, including English, French, and German. These languages have become a bridge linking the Palestinian Arabs with the West, facilitating the process of integration into Western societies.

Language is a means of communication. It is a reflection of and an introduction to a people's civilization and heritage. Hence the foreign language factor—all the more important because Palestine is a tourist country—became a two-edged sword for the churches, as it enriched as well as impoverished them, strengthened but also weakened them. It granted them new possibilities, but at the same time it stole from them their best children.

**d.** The fertility rate[11] is a factor of some importance. We have already demonstrated that the ratio of Christians living in Palestine to Christians abroad is roughly the same as the ratio between Muslims abroad and those in Palestine. But the birthrate among Christians is lower than that of Muslims, which affects the numbers.

The first three factors (demographics, social class, languages and continuity of contact with Western civilization) all affected the Palestinian Christians' outlook on life, influencing their view of marriage and number of children in a family in particular. Men married at a later age, there were fewer marriages, and numerous children were no longer considered a blessing or a means to achieve prosperity—despite the proverb that declares the child comes bringing his livelihood with him. Instead, numerous children were considered a heavy and nearly unbearable burden to the father. A Christian man no longer thought he could give his many children a proper education or adequate care, because it was more difficult to make a living and to preserve the existing standard of living. Hence Christians were satisfied with small families in comparison to their Muslim brethren, a fact supported by the statistics: In 1967, the fertility rate in Jerusalem was 4.1 percent, versus the Muslim rate of 5.3 percent; in the West Bank, the rate was 4.4 percent for Christians versus 5.0 percent for Muslims.

This means that the ratio of Christians to the total population is in continuous decline. The birthrate is too low to compensate for the high rate of emigration. The combination of emigration and low birthrate presents a frightful challenge to Christian existence in the Middle East in general, and in Palestine in particular.

This low birthrate is indeed a two-edged sword: on the one hand it is a cultural necessity in view of the world's population explosion. On the other hand, it is a great threat to the survival of Christian Arabs.

**e.** The orientation toward the West is a natural one. When Christian missionaries arrived in Palestine at the turn of the nineteenth century, conditions in the Ottoman Empire were very bad. Poverty, disease, and corruption were rampant. Health and education infrastructures were nonexistent. As a result of the West's industrial revolution, European social welfare institutions were just being established to solve the then widespread social problems abroad. Consequently the missionaries possessed an enormous amount of experience in organization and administration. They were interested in cleanliness and discipline. They founded schools, instituted programs of study, and built hospitals according to the specifications they had used in their own countries. They constructed huge buildings and introduced modern equipment unknown to the Palestinians under Ottoman rule.

Arabs in Palestine, Christians in particular, were convinced by all these factors that the Middle East was backward and the West was more important, generally more developed, and quite superior. Subconsciously they started to favor the West and all things foreign. In Europe, for example, the word *foreigner* has a negative connotation. Most people fear and resent foreigners and their alien traditions. But for most Arabs, and for Christian Arabs in particular, the word had positive connotations. They respected, loved, and served the foreigner, and considered foreign products superior to domestic ones. Thus Christians were drawn toward the West, which they viewed as a place of progress, civilization, and advancement.

Although this view of the West is changing somewhat—for example, Islamic movements are focusing on the moral decline of the West—

many Arab Christians still feel that the Middle East is far removed from development and advancement, and that the gap between East and West is widening, with Arab society destined to remain backward.

**f.** Arab Christians were among the first emigrants from the Ottoman Empire, forming a network in the New World which became one of the main enticements to the diaspora. Individuals who emigrated attracted their families, who in turn attracted other families, and so on. Consequently emigration is like a piece of cloth: if one thread is loosened, the rest unravel slowly but surely.

The emigration phenomenon of Christians in Palestine is an old one, although it gained special momentum toward the end of the last century when Palestinian Christian sections of cities and suburbs sprang up in the diaspora. These emigrant communities helped to attract more emigrants by providing housing, employment, and an atmosphere that eased the homesickness of new immigrants.

### 2. PSYCHOLOGICAL FACTORS
Along with distinctive social elements, special psychological ones figure in emigration.

**a.** Palestinian Christians are an inseparable part of the Palestinian Arab people, constituting 6.4 percent of the Palestinian people in the world, although they represent only 2.4 percent of the total population in the West Bank and Gaza Strip. They may be a quantitative minority, but not a qualitative one. Minorities face a greater threat from emigration than others for two reasons. First, the inferiority complex of minorities is linked to their fear of dissolution or fading away. They may also feel threatened by the majority. Second, the Middle Eastern countries lack a comprehensive democratic system that could have preserved pluralism and guaranteed human rights for individuals regardless of their religious beliefs, party affiliations, or political convictions. Individuals in the Middle East are not identified by their human but by their religious or party affiliations, which results in economic, political, and psychological consequences, such as inequality in employment possibilities, domination of one political party, and feelings of persecution.

**b.** Feelings of frustration and despair among Palestinians are engendered by the continuing Arab Israeli conflict, the failure to reach a just solution to the Palestinian question after more than fifty years, as well as the many economic crises, the lack of democracy, and an inferiority complex.

A frustrated Palestinian Muslim will often resort to religion and join the fundamentalist movements as a form of protest against the status quo. A frustrated Palestinian Christian will not resort to religion because of the historical Christian role in the development of nationalism. Instead, the Christian will opt for emigration, thus escaping from reality. Christian emigration, therefore, is not a reaction to the spread of fundamentalist Muslim movements.[12] It is instead a movement parallel to, and contemporaneous with, the fundamentalist movements.

## 3. EDUCATIONAL FACTORS

There are other factors that in my view have not been taken seriously enough. I am convinced, for instance, that emigration is closely connected to false educational concepts.

**a.** Caring for children is a sacred duty, but many Christian parents have the wrong idea of how to prepare their children for life. They are overprotective and take exaggerated care of their children, rendering them delicate and unable to bear much pressure. These children are unable to rely upon themselves. They become self-absorbed and fear to face hardship, even though all life is accompanied by hardship. Emigration is thus often one kind of escape from struggle and hard work.

**b.** Many negative aspects have adhered in religious education, due in large measure to the sectarian competition of the last century, which lured Christians to join one or another sect. This competition led to fearful consequences for Palestinian Christians. The individual sects pampered their members, supplying them with clothing, food, housing, schools, and even employment, all of which created a terrible dependence on them on the part of their members. As a result Christians grew up like pampered children receiving everything they asked for, believing they were masters born to be served by others. Rarely did these Christians believe that faith means sacrifice—sacrifice to build church and society, and to serve others. I say this with a heavy heart. As churches and pastors, we have raised a generation of consumers who have not learned responsibility and service, but instead have become dependent on the church and on the West. Consequently emigration was furthered by the impression that the West fulfills all human requirements not met at home.

## 4. RELIGIOUS FACTORS

**a.** In the context of our discussion we should confess that theology, the science that should bind Christian faith to the reality of life, is often a foreign and imported science unrelated to our daily Christian reality. It is a theology irrelevant to our circumstances, frequently expressed in a language foreign to the language of the country. Even the images in our churches portray Christ as a European with blue eyes and fair hair, as if he were English or German. This helps to create a subconscious feeling that Christianity is an imported Western faith, originating in the West.

A complicating factor is that texts like history books and catechisms do not touch on the Arab origin and roots of Christianity. As a result, Christians are rendered illiterate, ignorant of their deep Middle Eastern roots and their cultural roles in the history of Christianity. This alienation from their own roots and history is important in attracting Palestinian Christians to the West.

**b.** Until a short time ago, most Christian church leaders in Palestine were foreigners. Some still are. Some of these leaders were not interested in the Christians in Palestine at all. They concentrated on administering the holy sites and church properties in the country. Others consciously or unconsciously encouraged emigration to the West by failing to stress Christian steadfastness and Christian testimony in the East. It is noteworthy that the Arabization of many leaders in Palestine, such as Roman Catholic, Anglican, and Lutheran, was accompanied by a more widespread Christian presence in the Middle East.

All these factors helped to alienate the Palestinian Christians from their spiritual leaders and their church, thus helping to empty the church and increase emigration.

## Will Christians Disappear from the Holy Land?

The emigration of Christians from the Middle East in general and Palestine in particular is a disturbing phenomenon. It has had terrible political, economic, religious, and cultural consequences for Palestinian society in general and the Middle Eastern church in particular. If Christians disappear from Palestine, an essential part of our Palestinian people and an indigenous voice in the choir of our country's children will also disappear. A rich cultural element will be erased from the record of our Arab culture, and the bridge joining the East with the West will be destroyed.

If the Christians disappear from Palestine, much of the Holy Land will be transformed into ruins—churches and other buildings can be photographed but not attended as places in which to worship. They will be turned into amusement parks rather than sites of witness. For after all, the value of the land lies in its people and living stones, not ruins. The value lies in its faithful inhabitants, not its tourists.

If the Christians disappear from Palestine, the legacy of 1300 years of joint Christian-Islamic heritage will be lost—a heritage of coexistence, interrelationships, and peace that we have bequeathed to the world.

Yet there are some international and local developments that could stem the tide of Christian emigration and that could encourage Palestinian Christians to remain in their homeland. These developments are the unrest and civil wars in the Eastern European countries, the economic problems in the United States, and the racial extremism in Western Europe, all of which discourage emigration.

If the peace negotiations continue to be successful, a reasonable solution to the Palestinian problem will be achieved and a new Middle East order will be established to help investments, encourage the development of the economy, and utilize the natural and human resources in a democratic system. If this is achieved, then the future is here in the Middle East rather than in the West.

The Arabization of the Christian churches, which began with their leaders, has spread to include theology and education. This Arabization will eventually bind the faithful to their church, their society, and their country. At that point they will truly possess the power to be what the Master promised, "You are the salt of the earth and a light on a mountain."

# CHAPTER 3

# THE CRY FOR JUSTICE: THE PALESTINIAN ROAD FROM THE INTIFADA TO THE PEACE CONFERENCE

THE HISTORY of Palestine in this century is complicated, controversial, and hard to present impartially, and cannot be expounded in detail here. Although the present can be interpreted and understood only on the basis of the past, I intend to present only a socio-political analysis of the past five years, from the Intifada to the Peace Conference.

This kind of analysis is important if one wishes even to begin to understand the fate of the Palestinian people; but it is also necessary if one seeks ways to have justice prevail. Yet one must first explain the concept of justice more fully in theological terms, especially since Christians, in particular, often misuse it. I do not presume to be able to present the complete definition of this theological concept. Rather, I want to point out a few aspects of this concept, concentrating in particular on its relationship to law and power.

## Justice, Nothing but Justice

A particular relationship exists between justice, law, and power. They do not exist independently of each other but rather exhibit a very precise form of mutual interdependence. God gave the law as a framework within which the coexistence of human beings is ordered in such a way as to preserve life and at the same time prevent injustice (see, for instance, the Decalogue in Exodus 20:1–17). God also gave power to the governing authorities for the precise purpose of punishing evil and preserving and rewarding good (Rom 13:1–5).

Law and power are also linked in another way, for law needs power to enforce justice, and power needs law to prevent it from becoming unrestrained and thus an instrument of injustice, oppression, and exploitation. As a result, we can say that both law and power are intended by God to be servants of justice and protectors of law. That is the correct biblical relationship.

But the Bible also teaches us that the fall affected this relationship. Because of the fall, this relationship is in constant danger of degenerating and being perverted into its opposite. In that case the law becomes an instrument in the hands of the powerful: they enact it, they interpret it, and they enforce it. Those in power decide what is good and what is evil, what is just and what is unjust, what is useful and what is destructive. Abuse of law and of power become the order of the day. Law becomes the servant of the powerful, and justice becomes a football in the hands of the violent. That is how it is among sinning human beings, as it is presented in the Bible and known and addressed by Jesus when he tells his disciples, "You know that among the gentiles those whom they recognize as their rulers lord it over them, and their great ones are tyrants over them" (Mark 10:42). The Palestinian problem is the problem of a perverted relationship. It is a problem of unjust division of power, a problem of an unjust system that protects oppression and exploitation. It is the problem of law perverted to support the interests of the powerful and to satisfy their expansionist plans. At issue in the Palestinian conflict is the controversy between two radically conflicting interests. Whereas one side seeks to change the prevailing status quo of occupation, the other side tries to maintain it at any cost. The former suffers under the prevailing conditions, the latter profits greatly from it.

Under these circumstances, justice can mean nothing less than a radical redistribution of power, a reformation of the law as well as the abolition of unjust structures. Justice means nothing less than the reestablishment of the relationship between justice, law, and power so that power and law become the protectors and servants of justice. That is God's justice, of which Mary sings in the Magnificat, "He has shown strength with his arm; he has scattered the proud in the thoughts of their hearts. He has brought down the powerful from their thrones, and lifted up the lowly; he has filled the hungry with good things, and sent the rich away empty" (Luke 1:51–53).

Justice, therefore, is anything but impartial. What is at stake is taking sides in such a way "as to help the injured regain their rights and render the disturbers of the peace harmless, so that power may be distributed justly and the relationship reestablished in its original form, resulting in a state of maximal peace for all.[1] (A state of total peace is not attainable in this world. That is reserved for the eschaton.) This is what was at stake for the Palestinian uprising, called the Intifada, and this will hopefully be the result of the Peace Conference and the agreement concluded in 1993.

## The Intifada: The Cry for Justice

The Intifada[2] (Insurrection) of the Palestinians started on December 9, 1987—when no one expected it. The fate of the Palestinians had apparently been totally forgotten in 1987. No one in the world seemed to be interested in the Palestinians. The world was preoccupied with other things—the two superpowers with their disarmament conferences, the European nations with economic problems in the European Community, the Arab nations with the Iran-Iraq war, Israeli society with the domestic controversy between religious and secular Jews. Even the P.L.O. was concentrating on differences within the movement.

Moreover, the situation on the West Bank and the Gaza Strip seemed calm. An Israeli secret service report in 1987 confirmed that there was no reason to worry, since the Palestinians had become more or less reconciled to the Israeli occupation. The calm on the West Bank and the Gaza Strip was deceptive, resembling the calm just before a storm. The unexpected happened. The storm of Intifada broke out suddenly, unexpectedly, and unpredictably. No one knew whence it came, no one knew why it broke out just then. It raged first in Gaza, then spread quickly to the West Bank. And its effect was felt all over the whole world.

It all began with a "traffic accident" on December 8 at the Eretz crossing, the military roadblock where Israeli soldiers check all vehicles with Gaza license plates before they are allowed either to enter or to leave the territory of Israel. Some cars filled with Palestinian workers returning from work in Israel were waiting at this roadblock that day, as usual. An Israeli military transport truck suddenly crashed into these cars. Two cars were totally destroyed; four Palestinians were killed, and seven were severely injured. Three of the dead were from the Palestinian camp Djabalia. Djabalia is the largest refugee camp, with a population of more than 60,000 Palestinians who had been driven out in 1948 at the time Israel was created and who had since been living in extremely crowded, slum-like conditions.

The inhabitants of Djabalia considered this "accident" to have been an act of revenge against them for the stabbing of an Israeli businessman in Gaza the day before. The funeral of the three Palestinians in the refugee camp turned into a mass demonstration that continued on December 9. During this demonstration a fifteen-year-old child was shot in the heart by an Israeli soldier. He died the same day and became the first martyr of the "Intifada." Demonstrations quickly spread to the whole Gaza Strip and then the West Bank.[3]

This incident was not, of course, the cause of the Intifada. But it was the spark that set fire to a pile of dry tinder that had been accumulating for a long time. The suffering, fury, and hatred caused by twenty years of occupation suddenly exploded.

## The Occupation: A System of Injustice

Israel conquered the West Bank (including East Jerusalem), the Gaza Strip, a part of the Sinai Peninsula, and the Golan Heights in the Six Day War in 1967. Whereas the Sinai Peninsula was returned to Egypt in accordance with the Camp David agreement,[4] East Jerusalem and the Golan Heights were annexed by Israel in 1980 and 1981, in violation of all declarations of human rights, international laws, and United Nations resolutions.

The status of the West Bank and the Gaza Strip is a peculiar one: Israel neither annexed them nor obeyed United Nations Security Council Resolutions 242[5] and 338[6] demanding Israeli withdrawal. Instead, Israel has lived in a kind of common-law marriage with the Occupied Territories of the West Bank and the Gaza Strip. It was not (nor is it today) either properly married or properly divorced from the Palestinians living there. These Occupied Territories were neither incorporated into the Israeli "democracy," nor were they granted their independence and liberty. With the aid of its military might, Israel forced the Palestinians—against their will, and with no show of love whatever—to share its "bed." The Palestinians were thus raped daily by the Israeli military forces. This kind of common-law marriage satisfied the Israeli government's lust for expansion but proved loathsome and unbearable to the Palestinians. It brought economic advantage to the Israelis, but it brought oppression, exploitation, and dependency to the Palestinians.

Israel was and is today still interested solely in the land of Palestine, not in the Palestinians living there. Israel—in accordance with the old Zionist myth—still pretends that the land Palestine is a land without a people,[7] a land that has lain fallow and unpopulated for 2000 years, awaiting its ancient Zionist inhabitants. As a result, the Israeli policy is still based on annexing, confiscating, and incorporating ever more land, while preferably squeezing out (transferring) and exiling the people living there, or else using them for their own purposes. This is not only Zionist ideology, it is Israeli policy, and the Palestinians experience this policy day in, day out. It is this policy that led to the insurrection of the Palestinians.

The problem of Palestine is not a theoretical problem. It is the practical problem of a whole people prevented from living "normally" and deprived of their rights. Under the occupation, the Palestinian people have no right to vote; they are not permitted to participate in parliamentary elections; and since 1976 they are even forbidden to vote in local elections. In the local elections of that year the majority of Palestinians voted for candidates with close ties to the P.L.O. This did not please Israel, so no local elections have been held since. Several mayors elected in 1976 were murdered by Israeli radical rightists; others were exiled or removed from office by the Israeli military government.[8] Again and again it becomes obvious that Israel refuses to concede that, just as they themselves are a people, so are the Palestinians a people who desire to exercise the right of self-determination. They are not even allowed to choose their own representatives. There are always others who are convinced they know better and who decide for them.

Furthermore, living under the occupation means that Palestinians are not allowed control over the resources of their own country. Israel has already assumed direct control of over 65 percent of the territory on the West Bank and over 40 percent of the land in the Gaza Strip:

> There are many ways to bring land into Israeli control. The diversity, complexity, vagueness, and sometimes overlapping of these methods and their legal bases create a state of confusion probably not unintentional, and in any case highly welcome in Israel. The most important methods are: confiscation for military purposes; sealing off for military exercises; takeover of Jordanian public land; acquisition of the property of absentee owners through a trustee; dispossession for official purposes; declaration of non-registered land to be public domain; repossession of once Jewish land; purchase of land.[9]

The water resources of the Occupied Territories are under Israeli control too.[10] Eighty percent of these resources are placed at the disposal of the Israelis and their settlements. Palestinians are allowed the use of only 20 percent of their own water resources. Israelis manage a system of water pipes, but Palestinians in the Occupied Territories get "the water faucet" turned on perhaps once every two weeks, at which time they must fill their water tanks, from which they can then draw water until the next time the tap is turned on. The amount of water doled out in this way is maintained at a minimum level (the same level as 1967). That is how the Israelis keep the Palestinians in check and under their direct control. Moreover the Palestinians must pay a high price for water— four times as much as what an Israeli settler has to pay. This policy has catastrophic consequences for agriculture in Palestine, which is basically an agricultural country.

The occupation has also brought catastrophic consequences to Palestine's economy.[11] Israeli policy after the Six Day War was aimed at making the Occupied Territories dependent on the economy of Israel. Agriculture, industry, and the infrastructures on the West Bank and Gaza have remained underdeveloped. It was in Israel's interest to make of these territories a reservoir of cheap labor possessing no rights (until the Intifada, about half of working Palestinians were employed in Israel) as well as a ready market for Israeli products. The Occupied Territories were the second largest export market for Israel, after the United States. Israel finds Palestinians interesting only insofar as they are consumers of Israeli goods.

Israeli exploitation of the Palestinian population also took the form of keeping social welfare[12] to a minimum even while collecting large amounts of taxes. Welfare services like unemployment compensation and old-age pensions were denied to the Palestinians in the Occupied Territories. The condition of both health care and the educational system are deplorable to this day. Palestinians wanting a telephone must wait years to get it, if they succeed in getting one at all. Not much is done on road repairs unless the road serves settlers or repairs suit Israeli policy. What is appalling is that the humanness of Palestinians is not taken seriously. The Israeli military authorities consider their lives to have no particular value and treat them accordingly.

Moreover, Israel denies that Palestine is the homeland of the Palestinians. According to Israeli law, all Palestinians who were accidentally absent from the territories occupied by Israel in 1948 and 1967—perhaps on a trip, or in flight—lost their right to return to their homeland.[13] Israel is making it incredibly difficult for the Palestinians still living in the Occupied Territories today to maintain their right to Palestine as homeland. These Palestinians are instead viewed as aliens who happen by coincidence to be living in the Occupied Territories at the moment, and they are treated as though they did so only by Israel's grace. If Palestinians remain abroad from one to three years without returning to the Occupied Territories, they too lose their right to return to this homeland. What a life! And what a price is exacted when every Palestinian must return to his homeland every year so as to keep his right to his homeland! In contradistinction to this, Israeli law grants every Jew in the world the right to return to Palestine because one ancestor allegedly lived in Palestine 2000 years ago. The fact that Israel uses a double standard and exercises two kinds of law is nowhere as obvious as here.

This kind of treatment also becomes evident when one sees all the bureaucratic procedures a Palestinian must go through in order to settle civil affairs, such as registering with the various authorities or traveling to Israel or abroad. Conditions prevailing here resemble those prevailing in the Eastern Bloc during the Cold War. The queuing of Palestinians in front of the various Israeli agencies is just as bad and humiliating as was the queuing of the East Europeans in front of food stores.

Finally, to live under the occupation means that Palestinians are forced to live with no security under law, for only the Israeli secret service has the power.[14] The secret service's golden calf is "the security of the State of Israel," and for the sake of this security everything is permissible: arrests without charges or due process, torture, dissemination of drugs, extortion, and much more. Since the Israeli military government is the legislative, the executive, and even the judicial power, there is no objective and independent authority left to speak for the rights of Palestinians. The situation is aggravated by the fact that there are various laws in force in the Occupied Territories, including British Mandate laws, Jordanian laws, and the more than 1200 Israeli military statutes.[15] It is no wonder, then, that Israel picks and chooses among them to further its own interests. To make things worse, Israel does not consider the West Bank and Gaza Strip a part of the Occupied Territories but rather a no-man's land that it administers. Consequently the land itself is managed and annexed, but its people are displaced and deprived of rights.

## Justice for Two Peoples in Two States

It was more than twenty years of life under these conditions that led to the Palestinians' Intifada. For twenty years they had hoped for help from abroad—in vain. Now they intended to take charge of their own destiny. Now they intended to present their own case before the world. That was one goal of the Intifada that did succeed in large measure: the pictures and message of the Intifada transmitted by the world's media were undoctored. Palestinians succeeded in drawing the world's attention to their own plight. They were able to arouse sympathy for their cause.

Another goal was to force Israel to make a decision: Palestinians were in effect saying, "We find this common-law marriage unbearable. Either we get legally married, or we separate amicably. Either we, together with the Israelis, institute a democratic state where everyone has the same rights and obligations, or else we create two sovereign states that will exist side by side in peace." The first option was palatable, but Israel was strongly opposed to it. It wanted a state as purely Jewish as possible and at the same time democratic. But that would be attainable only if the non-Jews remained an almost invisible minority in the state of Israel. So if one chooses a democratic state encompassing both Israelis and Palestinians in the whole of Palestine, the pure Jewish state is jeopardized. At this point Israel feared above all the so-called population explosion caused by the high birthrate among Palestinians.

No wonder the majority of the Palestinians opted for divorce! They now wanted a Palestinian state that would exist alongside Israel in Palestine. "Two peoples, two states" was the motto of the Intifada from then on. This motto found its expression in the Declaration of Independence of the state of Palestine. The Palestinian National Council proclaimed the establishment of the state of Palestine on November 15, 1988. Due to its importance, this declaration is reproduced in its entirety in Appendix 1.

This declaration of the Palestinian National Council was the high point of the Intifada. Palestinians could use it to transform their Intifada into a political process. They used it to demonstrate their yearning, will, and readiness to arrive at a "just" and possible peace and their capacity to make compromises. This message rang throughout the world and achieved renewed sympathy, solidarity, and respect for the Palestinians. It forced the United States to begin a dialogue (albeit not a very honest one) with the P.L.O., for the Palestinians in the Occupied Territories wanted to "act" and the Palestinians of the diaspora wanted to "discuss."

Matters took an unexpected turn when the policy of "glasnost" was instituted in the Soviet Union, and the Eastern Bloc began to fall apart. The eyes of the world were suddenly turned in that direction. The Intifada continued, but it no longer attracted the attention it had once done. The world got used to the Intifada again. It would take a new crisis in the Middle East to redirect the attention of the world to the fate of the Palestinians. It would take the Gulf War.

## The Gulf War and the Peace Conference

It is still too early to arrive at a clear verdict about the terrible Gulf War. The war, however, clearly revealed the United Nations, the United States, and their allies could tolerate the occupation of Palestine but not of Kuwait. Palestine is merely holy; Kuwait, on the other hand, is oily.

But the world's double standard—really one single standard favoring the powerful and their special interests—which had become evident in the Gulf War was one of the factors leading to the Peace Conference in Madrid.

The Peace Conference, to which both the United States and the Union of Soviet Socialist Republics had sent invitations, started in Madrid on October 30, 1991. The conference was the result of eight trips into the region by then-Secretary of State James Baker. Participants in this conference were Palestinians, Jordan, Lebanon, Syria, and Israel, besides the European Community, Egypt, and the United Nations as observers, and a representative of the Gulf States.

The Palestinians went to Madrid with mixed feelings. On the one hand, they saw it as a chance that would not come again in the foreseeable future. They had the opportunity to present their cause anew to the world. On the other hand, many Palestinians doubted that Israel was seriously interested in a just peace. Israel's policy on settlements merely aggravated these doubts, which were further aggravated by the fact that the P.L.O. were prevented from sitting at the negotiating table.

The negotiations were separated into three phases: (1) the opening conference in Madrid, October 30–November 2, 1991; (2) direct negotiations between Israel and each Arab delegation, begun in Washington on December 10, 1991; (3) the multilateral negotiations to address issues of regional and international significance.

## The Treaty

Despite the negotiations and the election of a new government in Israel, the negotiations bore fruit only when a common interest was made apparent. As long as the East-West conflict had thrown its shadow across the Middle East, it was in the interest of all rulers of the region to avoid a definitive solution. But with the end of the Cold War, the rulers in the region realized that a continued lack of peace could only strengthen fundamentalism and allow its growth.

To the new government in Israel this meant that it would lose its power and that the religious conservative parties would again come to power if it failed to establish a lasting peace with its neighbors. And the P.L.O realized that a continuation of the status quo would only bring greater hopelessness and drive people into the arms of the fundamentalists. The rulers of Jordan, Syria, and Lebanon shared these fears, since a fundamentalist Islamic opposition was growing in these countries.

The new development led to a breakthrough in secret negotiations in Norway between Israel and the P.L.O. Two personalities in particular were decisively involved in the arriving at an agreement: Yasir Arafat and Shimon Perez.

Their breakthrough cleared the way for the festive signing of the so-called "Declaration of Principles in Internal Self-Government Arrangements" in Washington, D.C., on September 13, 1993, with President Bill Clinton.

The moment Arafat extended his hand to Rabin, the walls of estrangement collapsed and it became clear that a change in Palestinian-Israeli relations had occurred. A conflict lasting a century had come to an end. Both peoples realized that neither could conquer the other and that instead the fate of one cannot be separated from that of the other. And even more! Both peoples realized that at this historical moment they needed each other. Israel needed peace with the Palestinians so that it could establish relations with the Arab world, since no Arab state dared conclude a peace with Israel as long as the Palestinian problem remained unresolved.

On the other hand, the Palestinians needed peace with Israel. For one thing, they needed a pass giving access to the Western world and to rid themselves of the isolation they had suffered since the Gulf War. Israel, after all, is of central and basic significance for the West, above all because of the Holocaust. Their special relationship with Israel has made it almost impossible for Western nations to establish normal diplomatic and economic relations with the Palestinian people. Thus the signing of the treaty was a necessity and of advantage to both peoples.

Yet the problems have not been solved with the signing of the treaty. There are still occupied territories in which almost thirty years of occupation have resulted in negative developments. Many issues have not yet been resolved: the issue of Israel's borders, the issue of the establishment of an autonomous Palestinian state, and the issue of the final status of Jerusalem and of Israeli settlements. Proving the treaty successful is a task still ahead of us.

The greatest challenge to the Palestinians today is whether they are able to stand on their own two feet economically. If the Palestinians were to fail to develop a healthy economy of their own, they would see with their own eyes how Israel becomes a part of the so-called industrialized world while they themselves become part of the developing world. In that event, the conflict between Israel and Palestine, which was in part tied in with the East-West conflict, will become a part of the North-South conflict.

The greatest challenge to the whole Middle East will then be whether or not it is possible for the nations jointly to disarm and jointly to promote the democratization and economic development of their region in such a way as to create a kind of Middle Eastern community that the world could no longer underestimate either politically or economically.

# CHAPTER 4

# ARAB CHRISTIANS IN THE NEAR EAST: BETWEEN RELIGION AND POLITICS

THE THREE monotheistic religions originated in the Middle East. The whole history of this region would surely be quite different were it not for these religions, for they have shaped its politics, economics, literature, demography, philosophy, even its geography. The Middle East is also a region of many and constant ethnic, political, social, and ideological conflicts. Years of peace, prosperity, and progress have been rare here; war, poverty, and division have characterized the region.

Religion and conflict are thus distinguishing marks of the region, which raises the question whether they are related in any way. Was religion nothing but an attempt to flee from prevailing conflicts into a better and more exalted world? Do the three religions exacerbate or ease these conflicts in the Middle East? Will these religions be able to build bridges of understanding between people, or will they merely pour holy oil on a region already aflame?

It is precisely at this moment, when the groundswell of nationalism and fundamentalism is rising rapidly, that Christians are being asked to render an account of their faith. They are being forced to ask themselves whether and to what extent their faith can contribute to the solution of some of the burning social and political problems facing them. I shall dare to attempt a Christian Palestinian answer, taking this Christian minority's history and present circumstances into consideration. I shall search for some positive elements of the Christian faith that could be of assistance to the Middle East in the future.

## Arab Christians between Nationalism and Fundamentalism

The history of Christianity in the Holy Land is quite different from that of Europe. In Europe, Christianity spread and became the religion of the state, but, ever since the seventh century, Arab Christians have lived in an

Islamic world, where Islam was the state religion. As a result, Christianity was the religion of the minority, and Christians were tolerated as another "people of the book." As time passed, Islam developed the millet system in order to integrate Judaism and Christianity into the empire.[1]

*Millet* means "a community or a nation of people with a particular religion."[2] Islam gave every millet the right to use its own liturgical language, culture, and rites, as well as the right to maintain its own schools and courts.[3] The millet system was based on the "concept that law was personal rather than territorial, and that religion rather than either domicile or political allegiance determined the law under which an individual lived."[4] We can say that Christianity became a kind of ecclesiastical state within the Muslim superstate.

The Christians accommodated themselves to the new situation, learning that it is possible to forego political power. Even so, some Christians played important political roles during the Islamic eras.[5]

This isolation started to disintegrate at the beginning of the last century, with Napoleon's invasion of the Middle East. The first direct encounter between the Islamic world and the modern West took place in 1799. During the era of Muhammad Ali, in the nineteenth century, the Middle East experienced far-reaching changes,[6] three of which deserve mention here:

First, it became clear, as a result of the rebellion led by Muhammad Ali, that the Islamic world is not a homogeneous entity, but that it is comprised of various groups with special interests. The Arab-Turkish controversy came to the fore; European nationalism fell on fruitful soil in the Middle East, and was adopted by the Arab World, in order to free itself from Turkish yoke.

Second, a distinction began to be made between religion and state, faith and politics. The first ruler in the Arab world who tried to establish a state modeled on the West was Muhammad Ali. In 1832, he decreed that "Muslims and Christians are all our subjects. The question of religion has no connection with political considerations. [In religious matters] every individual must be left alone: the believer to practice Islam, and the Christian Christianity, but no one to have authority over the other. . . ."[7] This was the beginning of secularism in the Middle East, an idea alien to the traditional character of Islam.

Third, the encounter with the West took place at a time when the Ottoman Empire was suffering from extreme weakness. There was talk of "the Sick Man on the Bosporus," weakened by internal uprisings. Life in the Ottoman Empire was characterized by poverty, corruption, and lack of development. Europeans, on the other hand, apparently enjoyed prosperity. The European states seemed to be more progressive and to grow richer, manifested in part by the growing expansionism of these states into many parts of the Islamic world.

People in the Middle East began in the mid-nineteenth century to ask themselves, "Why is the Christian West experiencing such a boom while we remain so poor and backward? Could this have any relation to Islam or to the Muslims?" They started adopting Western intellectual values in an effort to escape the backwardness of the Ottoman Empire. Christians were drawn to the secular ideas of the West,[8] and dreamed of freedom and equality, for this was how they could find their way out of being a politically unequal minority. They joined with many Muslims in calling for a secular national state where Islam, though tolerated and honored, would no longer provide the norms of law and politics.[9] In that state Muslims and Christians would be able to stand on a completely equal footing.[10] Many Christian Arabs concluded that national unity was necessary in order to transcend religious differences.[11] They were convinced that, if state authority were not separated from the religious sphere, there could be no true civilization, no tolerance, no justice, no equality, no security, no freedom, no science, no philosophy, and no progress.[12] This kind of thinking transformed religion into a personal and intimate relationship between the individual and God, with no political implications, while land and nation were common to all. By calling for nationalism, secularism, and socialism, Christians were not just demanding equal rights. They were also calling for a new community in which they could take an active political part. The historical background makes it obvious why Arab Christians could not see any contribution that religion could make to benefit the future of the Middle East.

Islam now felt compelled to defend itself against this concept of religion. The Islamic reform movement was created in the second half of that century to defend Islam against the invasion of novel ideas, while at the same time it announced the dire need to reform Islam in order to provide a basis for a modern lifestyle.[13] The reformers rejected nationalism and imperialism but approved of the developments in the scientific field, as well as the Western style of art and culture.

This first reform movement, however, cannot be considered successful. In the first place, it did not represent a substantial part of the population but remained instead a movement strictly confined to intellectuals.

Second, the political upheavals caused by the outbreak of World War I and the collapse of the Ottoman Empire occurred in too rapid a succession for their ideas to spread.

During World War I, many reformers and numerous national movements supported the West, in hopes of attaining their independence from Ottoman rule. They strove toward realization of a pan-Arab empire. Changes brought about by World War I had a tremendous impact on the Middle East. A gigantic portion of what had previously been the Ottoman Empire came under direct Western control as huge areas were split into many small national states that were, however, still ruled by Western mandatory powers—England and France in particular. After the Versailles Treaty, the Arabs realized that they had been cheated by the West. They now understood that splitting the Ottoman Empire was not a temporary arrangement but rather a fact not easily revoked. Of the Ottoman Muslim Empire only Turkey remained independent. Under Kemal Attaturk, however, Turkey later divested itself of the foundations of an Islamic caliphate and turned to the West and its ideas, using force to ensure the process of secularization.

It took the Balfour Declaration (1917), announcing Britain's consent to the establishment of a Jewish homeland in Palestine, to awaken Muslims from their indifference. There arose a new brand of nationalism: the Syrians fought for a free Syria, the Palestinians for a free Palestine, and so on. Yet the idea of a great Arab empire was not abandoned. Here too, Arab Christians have played a leading part. Michel Aflaq, Antun Sa'Adeh, and others became the founding fathers of many secular Arab political parties, such as the Ba'ath party, the Syrian National Party, and others. Hoping to achieve equal rights and an improvement in their situation, these Christians even became adherents of the Communist parties of the Middle East.[14] Later, Christians also played a leading role in the secular Palestine Liberation Organization (P.L.O.) established in 1964. Mention should be made here in particular of George Habash, chairman of the Popular Front for the Liberation of Palestine (P.F.L.P.) and Naef Hawatmeh, chairman of the Democratic Front for the Liberation of Palestine (D.F.L.P.). The P.L.O.'s persistent and continuous struggle for a Greater Palestine was activated by its conviction that one should strive only for a secular state in which Jews, Christians, and Muslims enjoyed equal rights and coexisted in peace.

This turning toward the West and secularism was bound to arouse resistance from many Muslims, since it was tantamount to abandoning the idea of a Muslim empire. The Muslim Brotherhood was founded, the current ramifications of which can be seen in the group "Hamas." The Egyptian Hassan Al Bana[15] laid the foundation for this development in 1928 by emphasizing the close link between faith and creation, which is made manifest in Islamic society. He thus rejected any sort of secularism on the Western pattern, objecting especially to any kind of separation between religion and state. He stressed brotherhood and love. Notwithstanding the existence of many small states, the idea of an Islamic state should not be abandoned, he declared. All Muslims should be associated with one another in fraternal closeness and should strive for the actualization of the Muslim empire. He asserted that it was worthwhile for all Muslims to devote their lives to the Muslim brotherhood, above and beyond all national boundaries, and be willing to die for it.

The end of World War II inaugurated a new phase in the annals of the Middle East. Most Arab small states were granted their independence; revolutions brought native leaders to power, and most of them subscribed to nationalism, pan-Arabism, and socialism. There was great enthusiasm, and expectations were very high, as high as subsequent disillusionment was deep.

Yet these states were far from being genuinely independent. They were firmly enmeshed in the East-West conflict. In pro-Western countries, Islam was exploited as a stabilizing force supporting the ruling monarchies and an instrument against the danger of Communism. In pro-Eastern countries, one-party systems exercised a monopoly of power. Opposition parties were prohibited in both pro-Western and pro-Eastern countries. Here and there, the mosque remained the only meeting place not sponsored by the authorities.

But as governments started to use force against the Islamic movements within their boundaries by persecuting their leaders and throwing them into jail, they created martyrs. As a result, Islam began once more to raise its voice in the mid-1960s. The most important ideologist of that day was Sayyid Qutb,[16] who was murdered in 1966 on orders from the Egyptian president Gamal Abdel Nasser. Consequently he did not live to see the blossoming of the seed he had sown.

Qutb laid the foundations for today's Islamic fundamentalism in his book *Marks on the Road*. He started with the assumption that the time of ignorance ( *jahiliyya* in Arabic) not only existed in the period preceding Islam but also prevails in the Islamic world today. He maintained that human beings, Muslims included, do not recognize God's exclusive sovereignty. They forget that God is the only recognizable ruler through God's laws. Only the law is decisive. The motto from now on was *shari'a*, which is the Islamic term for law. Qutb declared that the cause of all problems known to the Islamic world may be the fact that the rulers do not act in accordance with these laws. The Islamic renaissance is extremely important because it leads humanity back to the sole recognition of God. Any ruler who does not adopt God's laws must be eliminated. The people themselves are to blame if an oppressor is in the seat of power. Qutb vehemently rejected a brand of Islam that restricted itself to the individual, insisting that society must be conditioned by the Qur'an, as God's word. One must dare to confront and destroy an oppressive ruler. Consequently, it is not surprising that Qutb attempted an armed uprising in Egypt and that Nasser suppressed it.

The year 1967 marks a new stage in the history of the Middle East. The defeat of the Arab nations in the Six Day War, followed by Israel's occupation of the West Bank and the Gaza Strip, was a great blow to Arab secularism. More and more people started to whisper that, although secular ideas had been helpful in the renaissance of Arab culture and in obtaining independence from the West, these ideas had failed to solve the economic and social problems of the region, including the most crucial problem, namely the Palestinian problem. Moreover, they had been unable to create real democratic systems in which equality, freedom, and human rights were guaranteed.[17]

While Arabs were turning away from secularism, many Israelis were calling the results of the Six Day War a wonderful act of God. Jewish religious enthusiasm and arrogance grew, and many Israelis started calling for a pure and expanded Jewish state.[18]

The Islamic and pan-Islamic movements of the region gained strength with the discovery that oil could be used as a political weapon, and with the outcome of the October War of 1973. Muslim conservatives and fundamentalists revived the idea of a Muslim state in which the Islamic *shari'ah* would be the determining factor. The Islamic Revolution in Iran demonstrated that, for the first time since the collapse of the Ottoman Empire in 1917, Islam was able to exercise control over all political, social, and economic aspects of a state.[19]

The failure of secular ideas to create a just, equal, and peaceful society, the emergence of Jewish religious fanaticism, and the rise of Islamic fundamentalism, as well as the collapse of the Soviet Union and Eastern Europe, have confronted Arab Christians with a great challenge.

Christians had clung to secular ideas separating religion from the state for 150 years. Now they were facing great movements that insist on unifying religion and state, wherein religion controls all aspects of life.

Is it time for a Christian fundamentalist movement? Is it possible to continue to cling to secular ideas? Or is there a way out of this dilemma by focusing on a certain religiousness in which Christians can work for a better future for all?

I believe that a contextual Palestinian theology is nothing else than an attempt to develop a local theology that is positive, relevant, and important for the future of the Holy Land. It is an alternative both to escaping into religious fundamentalism and to discarding religion for secularism.

## Agenda for a Christian Arab Theology in the Twenty-first Century

Several important aspects of a Christian theology in the Arab context will, in my opinion, gain significance in the coming years. They need to be examined in greater detail. These aspects challenge not only Christianity but Judaism and Islam as well. To face that challenge will be an important task for the three monotheistic religions.

**1.** Faith and politics must not be separated, especially in the Middle East. But they must not be blended, either. One must distinguish between them. The Middle East conflict is a political conflict, not a religious one. Consequently no "pious" solution, be it Jewish, Christian, or Islamic, is possible. Yet this does not mean that religion has nothing to say about the conflict. Religion is not only asked to contribute to a solution, its contribution is essential in the search for a political solution to the conflict. The Christian faith has an important contribution to make toward peace and justice in the region. One of the tasks of contextual Arab Christian theology is to define this contribution more clearly.

**2.** For the Christian contribution to be relevant, a thorough sociopolitical analysis of the conflict is absolutely necessary (see chapter 3). Such an analysis is important even to begin to understand the present. But it is also necessary if the theological statements are to do justice to the context. In the Kairos Document, the South African theologians declared, "It is not possible to make valid moral judgments about a society without having first made an attempt to understand that society."[20]

**3.** Contextual theology must redefine the concept of religion and give it content. In the Middle East (but not exclusively in the Middle East) the concept is often given a political content, in violation of the Second Commandment not to take the Lord's name in vain. God's name is also misused when God is used as a surrogate,[21] as, for example, when people who live in politically unstable and socially weak circumstances are driven to God as the last resort. In that event, religion becomes an escape in imagination out of the real world into a better, quieter, and more peaceful world. Fear, hopelessness, and frustration are used as whips to drive people to God—which really means to a particular political option, even if it appears in "nonpolitical" lamb's clothing.

Religion, properly understood, is a positive relationship between God and humans, simultaneously forming the basis for all of a person's relationships to other human beings and to the environment. That is why one must not undervalue the potential of faith and its significance to a person's "being in the world" or try to exclude it altogether. Yet "God wants us to comprehend him not in the unsolved questions but in the solved ones."[22]

Religion, incorrectly understood, directs the human being "in need to the power of God in the world,"[23] whereas true faith directs one "to the helplessness and suffering of God; only the suffering God can help."[24] Thus a contextual theology can only be a theology of the cross.

**4.** Contextual theology has to determine God's relationship to humans and to make the position of human beings in religion clear on that basis. A theology of creation can be very important to us in the Middle East, where several religions, as well as nations, coexist. Such a theology holds that all human beings, no matter what their religion or nationality, are created in the image of God. To protect a human being's rights is therefore a divine law.

For us Christians, the Incarnation plays an important role in better defining a human being. God became human in Christ and thereby gave divine significance to all human life. That is why racism, fascism, and religious fanaticism are alien to every true religion. Since the Incarnation one can no longer use religion against human beings or pit God against human beings. It must obviously also be impossible since the Incarnation to wound, discriminate against, or even make war against human beings in the name of God. If a human being is wounded, then God is wounded also. If a human being is honored, God is too. Whoever loves God also loves the "brother or sister" (1 John 4:19–21). To be religious, therefore, means simply to be a true human being.

**5.** Land remains a problem in the Middle East. The Occupied Territories are the specific causes of controversy between Israel and the Palestinians, or rather between Israel and the Arab nations. A contextual theology must emphasize the sacredness of God—which means that of humans also—not the sacredness of land. Yet land is one of God's gifts to humanity, meant to be lived on and to be shared justly. A resolution to the conflict will be possible only when the land is equitably divided between the Israelis and the Palestinians. Only in that way can both peoples live in freedom, dignity, and sovereignty. There is therefore a very particular relationship between a human being and land: sometimes one must renounce land in order to attain one's humanness; and sometimes one must cling to the land in order not to lose one's humanness. The land was created for humans, not humans for the land; and the task of every prophetic theology that has justice as a criterion is to understand this and expound this distinction.

**6.** Jesus quoted the prophet Isaiah (Isa 61) in the synagogue in Nazareth, and applied the passage to himself, saying he was "to bring good news to the poor . . . to proclaim release to the captives and recovery of sight to the blind, to let the oppressed go free" (Luke 4:18). As a result, every religious contribution contains a deep sense of identity with the poor, the weak, and the oppressed. It is for this reason that, already early on, the churches of the Middle East founded hospitals, rehabilitation centers, orphanages, retirement homes, and other social institutions. In the Middle East, social mission is one of the church's most important contributions. Welfare services, however, are not enough. Christians realize that poverty and oppression are not "coincidences but are rather the result of a conscious policy to increase the wealth and power of others."[25] A positive Christian contribution must take this into consideration and must continue to act until a new, just economic and democratic system has been established. After 1967, and even more so after 1987, the church therefore also began to align itself on the side of the politically oppressed.

**7.** One look at the political landscape of the Middle East suffices to show that it lacks any sign of logic. The policies of most of the Arab nations—but those of Israel as well—often appear to be irrational, incalculable, and incomprehensible. And religion too often appears to be "magic," naive, and even fabulous.

That is precisely why knowledge, information, training, and education are important to every contextual theology. Every exercise of political as well as religious power and authority must therefore "serve God's purpose for this world and be held responsible by the person in whose name it occurs."[26] Both politics and religion need responsible knowledge to prevent their becoming naive, fanatic, or irrational. It is for this reason that the work of the Middle Eastern Christian churches in elementary, secondary, and college education is of great significance to the future of the region. A "thoughtful faith" is what is needed here.

**8.** A contextual theology must clarify its relationship to its own culture. Christianity is not an eternal law but rather a faith—in space and time—in the God incarnate in space and time. The context of Christian Arabs is the Arab-Islamic space. Arab Christian faith and Arab Islamic culture have influenced and enriched each other with the passage of time. By achieving this clarification, Arab Christians could make a genuine contribution to the universal church.

**9.** The Middle East is home to many Christian confessions. Consequently a contextual theology has no choice but to be ecumenical, for the teeming problems in the region challenge every church without exception. As a result, there cannot be too great a disparity in the solution to these problems, which can only be tackled through teamwork.

This short agenda is a challenge to all the Christian confessions living in the Middle East, as well as to the other two monotheistic religions. A dialogue between all people of goodwill is essential, constituting a chance to arrive at a condition of maximum justice, stability, and development in the region.

# CHAPTER 5
# DAHER'S VINEYARD

DAHER WAS an Arab Christian from Lebanon. He and his family left Lebanon at the beginning of this century and settled in Bethlehem. He wanted to start a new life there. Since he was a farmer, he bought a piece of land of about 420 dunums (forty-two hectares) in the vicinity of Bethlehem with the money he had brought with him. The land was about ten kilometers south of Bethlehem, 950 meters above sea level on one of the hilltops in the Jewish mountains. One had a great view to the West from there; on a clear day, one could even see the Mediterranean.

The whole region was known for its vineyards. After all, it was not far from where the Israelite scouts sent by Moses had returned with a single cluster of grapes so large it took two men to carry it (Num 13:23). Daher began to cultivate his land with his two sons. It was full of stones, thorns, and thistles. It took a lot of hard, sweaty labor to clear it. They planted thousands of small trees: grape vines, pomegranates, almonds, figs, and olives. The land became a small paradise for Daher and his family, but one that needed constant care and preservation if it was to bear fruit.

It was an inexhaustible joy to all of them to behold the fruits of their own labor. The whole family would move out to the fields every day; father, mother, sons, and daughters all participated in the work as well as the harvest. During harvest time the family even spent their nights in a cave on their land. They would light a fire in the evening and sing songs, tell stories, and finish with a small devotional service. When the harvest was over, the family returned to Bethlehem, where they sold most of their crop, allowing them to live on their earnings from the sale.

That lasted a long time. But then the unexpected happened. Toward the end of the 1920s the conflict between Jews and Arabs in Palestine began to cast its long shadow. By the end of the 1930s the situation had degenerated to such an extent that it hurt the Daher family. The out-break of World War II and the Arab-Israeli war shortly afterward did not improve matters. But it could not break the family's ties to their land.

Daher's sons had meanwhile grown up. After the truce in 1949, one of Daher's sons decided to move onto the land to be on the site, to farm the fields, and to watch over the fruit trees. The land of his father was so important to him that he was willing to give up a comfortable life in Bethlehem, move out to live in a cave far from town, and face many dangers. He even stayed unmarried. His land became his life's companion; he lived with it for thirty-five years. Only death could sep-arate him from it.

Eventually Daher's other son, an evangelist, also died, leaving his wife and nine children, the youngest six years old. It was impossible for the widow and her children to cultivate all of the land. They had no money to buy new farming equipment. But because the land was so im-portant to them, they tried as well as they could to cultivate and preserve the inheritance of their fathers. Their goal was some day to farm all of it, and they awaited the moment they could realize that goal.

It did not turn out that way. In October 1991, Daher's grandchil-dren learned by accident that the Israeli military government intended to confiscate thirty hectares of their land. The reason given: the land had lain fallow for some time. This may sound logical to Western ears, for the myth that Israel had transformed this "Palestinian desert" into a "green oasis" still survives in the subconscious of many Westerners. If one heard the Israelis' reason for confiscating Daher's vineyard, one would think that Israel was trying to use the land and to reclaim it. Yet the Is-raeli military was suppressing the following important facts:

**1.** It is impossible for the Daher family to obtain the water neces-sary to cultivate all the land, since the Israelis have limited the Pales-tinians' water allotment to the minimum level (close to the 1967 level). Furthermore, Israel reserves almost 80 percent of the water in the occu-pied territories for its own use. For the 20 percent remaining to the Pales-tinians, they must pay four times the price. If Israel grants to the one mil-lion Palestinians living on the West Bank about 137 million cubic me-ters of water, it makes about 100 million cubic meters available to the Israeli settlers on the West Bank and the Gaza Strip. Thus every settler receives nine times more water than the Palestinians.

But how can the Palestinians develop their agriculture under these circumstances? They can plant only the kind of fruit trees that need only the rain to water them. Daher's vineyard had been planted with this kind of tree. Yet every day, whenever the Daher family went out to work on their land with their own hands, and whenever they looked over the fence to the neighboring vineyard, they were reminded what it means to be a Palestinian. Over there, only 500 meters away, was the Israeli settlement with the biblical name "Daniel's oasis." The Israeli government provides these settlers—who live on land confiscated from Palestinians—with everything they need: water, land, money, electricity, bulldozers, and tractors. No wonder these settlements are blooming while Daher's vineyard looks wilted.

**2.** If one thinks about it, the real reason for confiscating the vineyard is obvious. The Daher family's vineyard occupies a lovely hilltop surrounded by three Israeli settlements. This vineyard is a thorn in their side. It is the goal of some of the larger religious organizations (for example, the Amana Movement of Gush Emunim, the Herut-Betar Movement of the Herut party, and the Ha'oved HaLeumi of the Likud party) to confiscate this vineyard and establish another settlement for the religious conservative-extremist Jewish settlers. Those organizations are officially supported by the Israeli government as well as by the leading international Zionist organization. Their appetite for land knows no limits, not even the limits imposed by human life and human rights.

The Daher family came to me with the Israeli military order to confiscate the vineyard in hand. I read it. I cannot say I was totally surprised. What was clear to me was that the Israeli government was following a biblical tradition set by King Ahab and his wife Jezebel (1 Kings 21).

Ahab, king of Samaria, had a palace in Jezreel. But Ahab was not satisfied with the large and beautiful palace. He coveted the vineyard of his neighbor Naboth. Ahab wanted Naboth's vineyard at any price. First he offered him "a better one." But he was also ready to pay him with silver. In vain. Naboth did not want to give away his ancestral inheritance. To keep this inheritance was something like a divine command to Naboth. This attitude still exists in many Palestinians. To them the land is as important as their life. To sell it amounts to a betrayal of their ancestors and a scandal. Naboth knew that very well. That is why he did not want to give away his vineyard.

But Ahab also knew that, as king of Israel, he had no right to confiscate the land of an Israelite farmer, just as David had no right to kill Uriah the Hittite in order to have Uriah's wife, Bathsheba. In accordance with faith in Yahweh, even the Israelite kings were subject to divine law.

But Jezebel, the Sidonian king's daughter, had a different faith (worship of Baal) and thus a different understanding of royalty. That is why she asked her husband whether he was really still king of Israel when he did nothing about Naboth's refusal. Jezebel's models were the Canaanite city kings, who were absolute sovereigns. It was the master-subject relationship that was decisive to the Canaanites, not the "relationship of brothers." They thought that the law served the king and his desires, rather than serving God.

So Jezebel asked for two scoundrels to bear false witness against Naboth, saying, "You have cursed God and the king." The security of God and state were of uppermost importance. Naboth was stoned to death, and Ahab was then free to confiscate all his possessions.

I was immediately reminded of that story when I heard about the planned confiscation of the Daher family's vineyard. I was sure that the reason given for dispossessing them was a lie, but it would result in lending the state's act a spurious legality. In truth, dispossessing Palestinians of their land serves the ambitions of Zionist expansion policy. God, the promise of land, the security of the state of Israel, and alleged concern about fallow land are nothing but "holy means" to facilitate carrying out an "unholy policy."

Today's state of Israel, with its plan to dispossess Palestinians of their land and its policy of establishing settlements, is in the tradition of Jezebel, and that means that it is not in the tradition of the God of Israel. It is instead the tradition of "alien gods." The present Israeli policy could be likened to whoring around with other gods. It is a regression into Canaanite customs, where the desires of the state know no bounds and the laws are bent accordingly.

But that should not be the case in Israel, for it was here that what counted was that law, and possession, and above all the life of the individual before God were, without exception, secure. That is why God's messenger should appear to intervene wherever an obvious injustice is committed, wherever God's commandment is violated and whenever the court is misused to condone murder—when no one who is appointed to guard the law does so. The office of prophet in all of the Old Testament is that of intervening wherever a responsible authority breaks down.

Persons and institutions who are in this prophetic tradition cannot keep silent in the face of Israel's policy of land confiscation. Nor can the church of Jesus Christ, which honors the prophetic inheritance, avoid intervening when a nation—even if it is Israel—abuses its mandate. If the church does not intervene, it itself becomes culpable and discredited.

Therefore we, as the church, could not fail to act with regard to the expropriation of Daher's vineyard. We were forced to attempt to prevent it; we therefore started a drive with the participation of Christians of various denominations, Muslims, and Jews from the peace movement. Several committees were set up.

The first committee was delegated to deal with the legal implications. A lawyer, who was a member of the congregation, went to court to appeal the expropriation order, for we had been granted forty days to do so. Our position was not a bad one at the outset, since the Daher family could produce all the necessary documents proving their ownership, from the British Mandate authorities as well as from the Jordanian and Israeli governments.

Another committee was ordered to procure a tractor as soon as possible so that the land could be plowed quickly. With the help of the church and several German friends, we were able to raise the money to buy a used tractor. We drove the tractor to the vineyard to start cultivating. But scarcely had we started work than soldiers appeared and told us that we were not permitted to farm the land. They gave no reasons. They simply said if we wanted a reason we should apply to the military governor of the Israeli settlement of "Gush Ezion." But we could not give up that easily.

A third committee was given the task of procuring a variety of plants and of planting them in the vineyard. We succeeded in getting and planting 1700 young cabbage plants, 200 olive trees, and more than 1000 almond and plum trees. The planting was done by Christians, Muslims, and Jews, as well as Europeans and foreigners. It served as a symbol of solidarity with all the Palestinians whose land is threatened with confiscation.

A fourth committee was delegated to establish communications with the media (newspapers, television, periodicals) and interested groups (foreign embassies, churches, agricultural organizations) and to provide them with reports of developments.

A fifth committee was to conduct a study with the help of an agronomist on how one could make the best use of the vineyard to provide an income not only for the Daher family but for others as well, especially the unemployed. The idea was to make it a congregational pilot project for the community.

A sixth committee was asked to develop a study on how one could establish a Christian Palestinian village on that land. The Daher family is prepared to make the necessary land available to the congregation. The idea was to build housing for those Christian families who had lost everything they had in 1948, had come to Bethlehem, and now lived in inadequate housing and therefore often played with the idea of emigrating.

The matter is still unresolved. Will the Daher family be able to keep the vineyard of its forefathers, or will it be confiscated and turned into an Israeli settlement? Will the state of Israel give ear to the whisperings of Jezebel and her successors, the settlers, or will it hear the words of the prophets? The future of Israel depends on its decision.

PART 2

# On Interpreting the Bible in the Israeli-Palestinian Context

# CHAPTER 6
# A PERSONAL PERSPECTIVE

I COME FROM A Christian Palestinian family. My parents were members of the Evangelical Lutheran congregation in Bethlehem; both were pious Christians. Holy Scripture was not extra or ornamental to them. It was a lifetime companion, a basic necessity. Bible reading was part of our daily routine at home. We read all of Holy Scripture, the Old Testament as well as the New Testament.

The Bible was also familiar through children's services and youth work. I can still remember the time we children, with bated breath, walked along with Joshua seven times around the city of Jericho. And when we heard about the walls tumbling, we cheered, clapped, and danced. We thought that we, the Christian Palestinian children in Sunday school, were truly the conquerors of Jericho.

And I still remember when we in the youth group read the story of David and Goliath. We were unanimous in our sympathy for David. He was to us a model for the daring of faith and the courage of trust in God. The fact that Goliath was a Philistine and David an Israelite didn't bother us a bit. We identified totally with David the Israelite, because we put him and Joshua in the same line as Jesus. If Joshua and David had not won, Jesus would perhaps not have been born. Joshua and David were spiritual figures to us, not political ones at all. They were like saints to us—symbols for our religious struggle.

I grew up with these biblical personalities. And, because the Bible meant so much to me—indeed, it shaped my identity—I decided to study theology. I am not exaggerating when I say that I knew almost the whole Bible by heart. But I wanted to know my Bible better, understand it better, and explicate it better through more careful exegesis.

But there was not a single theological school in Palestine, so I was forced to travel abroad. I received a scholarship from the Lutheran World Federation and began my theological studies in Germany.

I began my studies in Germany with the conviction that biblical studies were not something one learned only at a university but rather something one should have learned at home. My desire was ultimately to learn to know Jesus better, and to learn more about Joshua and David. But my problems started with the "wanting to know more," for this started a process of alienating me from my Bible. The Joshua and David so familiar to me suddenly became politicized, somehow no longer seen in continuity with Jesus, as they used to be. They were instead placed into a kinship with Menachem Begin and Yitzhak Shamir. Their conquests were no longer for spiritual values but for land—my land in particular.

My Bible now showed an aspect previously unseen by me. The Bible I had heretofore considered to be "for us" had suddenly become "against us." It was no longer a consoling and encouraging message to me but a frightening word. My salvation and that of the world were not the issue in the Bible any longer. The issue was my land, which God had promised to Israel and in which I no longer had a right to live unless it was as a "stranger." The God I had known since my childhood as love had suddenly become a God who confiscated land, waged "holy wars," and destroyed whole peoples. I began to doubt this God. I started to hate this God and quietly became "indignant at God, if not with blasphemy at least with great grumbling."[1]

But I was more indignant at the theology professors who disseminated this kind of teaching. To them Israel was first of all a holy and mysterious people, a suffering people oppressed by every other people, a people worried about its survival yet miraculously beating its powerful foes. It seemed to me that many German theologians had become infected with the "Israel craze" after the Six Day War. As a Palestinian, I, on the other hand, noticed very little of Israel's suffering or holiness, even when I heard about the oppression of Jews.

To me, Israel was first and foremost a well equipped army of occupation, which had occupied my land and which held a defenseless people oppressed. This side of Israel, with which I was confronted every day at home, was seldom mentioned publicly in Germany. The uncritical and ahistorical equation of today's state of Israel with biblical Israel, the theologians' shock over the Holocaust, and Israel's victories over the Arab states had led some Western theologians to spiritualize the state of Israel.

## Theology after Auschwitz and the Palestinians

Many Western Christians and theologians could begin to understand today's Judaism and the modern state of Israel only through the Holocaust. It was the task of the so-called post-Auschwitz theology[2] to investigate the Holocaust theologically. Post-Auschwitz theologians were surprised to discover that the anti-Semitism prevalent in Europe had Christian roots, among others, and so they set out to expose and uproot it.[3] Their task was the more urgent when nothing self-evidently new emerged after 1945—anti-Semitic roots went very deep indeed.

This theology initiated a new phase in Christian-Jewish dialogue. In Europe and North America many organizations were established to devote themselves to this dialogue and to search for a new relationship to Judaism and the state of Israel. Yet this dialogue—which must be acknowledged as an important and progressive step in Western Christian theology—failed to achieve two things.

First, in the West, it failed to attract large numbers of participants. The dialogue has remained more or less the business of experts.

In Israel, the possibility of obtaining interested dialogue partners was quite limited. Very few Jews have even heard of such a dialogue; only a few individuals have participated in any way. Consequently this dialogue has, to a large extent, remained an intra-Christian Western monologue. Moreover, Western theologians never even consulted the Christians in the Middle East, to say nothing of drawing them into the dialogue. The Christian-Jewish dialogue, in its Western form, became so absolutized that the English-speaking theologians left the Arab Christians no alternative but either to adopt the Western viewpoint or be branded as nationalists and frivolous theologians.

A second problem with Jewish-Christian dialogue was that it barely even noticed the fate of the Palestinians, to say nothing of attempting to deal with the injustice done to Palestinians especially by the United States, by Europe, or by Israel. As a matter of fact, the "dialogue" never really saw the state of Israel in its total reality. That is, the history of Israel in the second half of this century relating to Palestinians and their expulsion and occupation was not taken seriously, nor was it included in theological thinking.

Post-Auschwitz theology asked how one could speak of Jesus Christ without becoming anti-Jewish. The answer was to emphasize henceforth the Jewishness of Jesus in Christology.[4] But in some people this gave rise to a pro-Jewish stance linked to an uncritically pro-Israeli stance. The result was that Israel was mythologized in this dialogue; the obverse of this was nothing less than a demonizing of "Palestinians" and the P.L.O. Pre-Auschwitz Christology had indeed contained anti-Jewish traits, but post-Auschwitz Christology often led to a pro-Israeli, anti-Palestinian stance. Consequently, if post-Auschwitz theology considers how one must speak of Jesus Christ without becoming anti-Jewish, it should in the same breath consider how one can speak of the Jewishness of Jesus without becoming anti-Palestinian. These questions are inseparable.

One more factor must be considered in an examination of Auschwitz and the Holocaust, namely the relationship of theology to power and to the powerless. One of the basic problems in the Third Reich was that the so-called theology of the German Christians identified itself with the ideology of the powerful. Instead of interpreting God's justice in their own situation, and thus helping the oppressed (Jews and non-Jews) obtain justice, German Christian theologians became instruments of the state, defending and justifying its actions and propagating its ideology. That is why they also failed to place themselves on the side of the powerless and to protect those whose rights had been taken away.

Post-Auschwitz theology saw the poverty of this theology and wanted to return theology to its rightful place, that is, totally on the side of those deprived of both power and their rights, rather than with those on the throne of the mighty. In the Third Reich, the deprived were Jews, among others, which is why post-Auschwitz theologians declared that the debt owed to the Jews should be discussed and a new relationship should be established with the victims or their families and descendants.

But the situation had already changed by the time post-Auschwitz theology started this task. The Jews no longer lived in Europe. They had won for themselves a state in Palestine. Their own experiences with helplessness had made them "power mad." The very Jews once deprived of power were transformed—with the backing of the wealthy and influential Jews in the United States—into the mighty state of Israel, a state having the best-equipped army in the region, the most modern war machines, even atom bombs.[5] In my opinion, post-Auschwitz theology did not pay enough attention to this change in the Jews' power. At the time this theology started to deal with the debt to the Jews, Israel was in the process of discriminating against the surviving Arab minority and treating Palestinians as second- and even third-class citizens. It later conquered the Arab armies and occupied the West Bank and Gaza and so held a whole people defenseless and powerless against their will, refusing to grant them human rights and independence. Yet post-Auschwitz theology has had nothing to say on this issue.

## Palestinian Christians and the Bible

Palestinian Christians suffering daily under the occupation can neither keep silent about Israel's actions nor rise above them theologically. Indeed, their context forces them to face new theological challenges instead. Christians in Palestine had a particular way of interpreting the Bible until the middle of the last century. All the churches interpreted Holy Scripture allegorically or typologically. They saw a deeper meaning, one that applied to Christ, in the texts of the Old Testament. The events and figures sketched in the Old Testament were images and foreshadowings pointing beyond themselves toward the future and the real. They were handed down to us for the sake of that future and that reality.

That way of interpreting the Bible started to change after the end of the last century. The Bible became a political text at the moment the Zionist movement promised itself the land of Palestine. The Old Testament promises became problematic for the Palestinians the moment the Jews promulgated their settlement of Palestine as their return to the land of their forefathers.[6] Palestinians were confronted with a new challenge the moment the state created in 1948 was named Israel.

Palestinians were now forced to seek new ways of interpreting Scripture.[7] They could no longer interpret the Bible allegorically. So they started to investigate ways they could interpret it in their own political context. The task was the more urgent as many Western Christian theologians had given the state of Israel a theological significance. How then could Palestinian Christians read their Bible? If they read it allegorically, it did not have much to say to them. If they read it politically, its message was frightening.

In this light, some aspects of scriptural interpretation are important to the Israeli-Palestinian context and are of significance to both an intra-Christian Western-Palestinian dialogue and a Jewish-Christian one.

**1.** The Bible is God's Word in human words. The writings of the Old and New Testaments are the records and written accounts of various experiences human beings have had with the one God. They are nothing but testimonies of faith. Those affected had a chance to speak, which is why these writings do not contain objective facts but rather experienced truths. The theme of the Bible is not God as such, but rather God's coming to humans and how these humans have experienced this coming. The Old Testament is the record of Israel's history with God. The New Testament is the witness of the disciples to the God who appeared in Jesus Christ. Neither testament is a reproduction of facts meant to preserve these experiences; instead, they aim to allow others— everyone, if possible—to share these experiences and identify themselves with them.

A statement of faith always contains an invitation. The story of God's dealings with Israel was written down so that the children of Israel could get to know their past and participate in it. The thrust of the Old Testament already was to make the story of God's dealings with Israel available to the Gentiles, meaning the other peoples. And God's promise to Abraham, like a prospectus, is at the very beginning of this story: "And in you all the families of the earth shall be blessed" (Gen 12:3).

We Palestinians are not excluded from this promise. Rather, we are drawn into it and invited to identify ourselves with the God of Israel. We Christian Palestinians can do this because Jesus Christ comes to us from the God of Israel and appropriates God for us without, however, dispossessing "the others."

**2.** Holy Scripture did not fall from heaven and is not timeless. It is written in history, it is history, it makes history. Every writing in the Bible originated in a specific context and relates to a context that must always be taken into consideration. This is necessary for the sake of the context itself as well as for its content, for there is no such thing as a text without a context. Typological and allegorical interpretations are neither relevant nor helpful in exegesis. We must ask ourselves with every text, "When was this text written? By whom, for whom, for what purpose, why, was it written? How was it used, and where does it belong?" Socio-historical investigations should be included in responding to these historical-critical questions.

As Christians, we recognize that our faith originated in a Jewish context—theological as well as historical—and that we have roots in common with the Jews. But we cannot stop there. I think we have to go further and recognize that Islam, too, is included in this Jewish-Christian context, theologically as well as historically. We have things in common with Muslims too. Just as Judaism is a part of the Christian history, so Islam is a part of the history of the effects of Christianity. Any theology in the Palestinian context therefore has the duty to examine this history of effects and the convergences as well as differences of these three Abrahamic religions.

The biblical texts not only have a history; they have given rise to history and made history; and every exegesis must take that into consideration. It cannot be denied that certain biblical texts have played an abysmal role. Passages have often been dragged in to justify anti-Semitism; and very often the Bible has been cited against the Palestinian people and their right to land and life. These examples of historical effects must be exposed and used as a warning that any interpretation of the Bible must be held accountable to God and human beings.

Every theology needs to encompass the history of the effects of texts, so that none can maintain the illusion of being an absolute and timeless theology. Every theology really grows out of a specific history of specific effects and is therefore related to a context. All theologians need to be warned that there is great danger when their theology is unaware of its relation to its context, and they imagine they can disseminate eternal verities without a context. The various contexts do not exist alone, independent of all others; they influence each other in an organic relationship. Consequently it is essential to have dialogues between the various contexts.

When interpreting a text today, or when making a theological declaration, one must ask oneself what that text means in its present context. How is it being understood? What does it accomplish? What effects could it have? For one and the same declaration can be interpreted in different ways in different contexts and can therefore have different meanings. One and the same theology can produce contradictory effects. It could mean either salvation or damnation, liberation or enslavement, justice or injustice, peace or war. That is why one must pay attention to the social, economic, and political implications, the motives and interests, that play a role in every exegesis.

**3.** The Bible is always contemporary. It is a living thing and cannot be put up in a jar. God's Spirit brings Scripture home to us; God brings it close. But this Spirit of God does not yield to our whim; it is bound to Scripture, and only faith makes it possible. No interpretation that excludes faith is possible. One can interpret Scripture correctly in any given context only when one's conscience is illumined by faith and one's reason is permeated by love.

**4.** The Bible is a great whole. The Old Testament and the New Testament form a unity. For us Christians, the Old Testament without the New Testament is not enough. But the New Testament without the Old Testament will either be misunderstood or not understood at all. The New Testament enlarges the horizon of the Old Testament and makes a correct interpretation possible. But the New Testament can be seen as a particular interpretation of the Old Testament, disclosing the correct understanding of the Old Testament. The New Testament without the Old Testament would be in danger of being spiritualized. The Old Testament can make us see the connection of socio-political realities to faith.

This unity is grounded in God's very self, for the God of Israel is the Father of Jesus Christ. It is the one and the same God. In both the Old Testament and the New Testament this God is a God of justice.

**5.** Holy Scripture is the book about a minority. The Old Testament is the faith experience of a Jewish minority in a non-Jewish world; the New Testament is the faith testimony of small Christian communities in a pagan Roman world. Persecution is a part of the experience of minorities. Thus the Bible is also a book about persecuted people, written by persecuted people.[8] Most of the authors of Holy Scripture were persecuted—one need think only of the Old Testament prophets or of Paul or of John in the New Testament. One can see that many of these works were written in exile, in prison, or in deadly danger. It is also worth noting that the most important figures in Holy Scripture were persecuted—not just Moses, but also "Gideon and Barak, Samson, Jephthah, David and Samuel and the prophets" (Heb 11:32). "Others suffered mocking and flogging, and even chains and imprisonment. They were stoned to death, they were sawn in two, they were killed by the sword; they went about in skins of sheep and goats, destitute, persecuted, tormented—of whom the world was not worthy. They wandered in deserts and mountains, and in caves and holes in the ground" (Heb 11:36–38).

Other Old Testament figures, who had not known persecution and who, interestingly enough, were not mentioned by the author of Hebrews—Joshua and Saul, for example—are somewhat problematical. They appear as warriors and conquerors who have received God's command to "utterly destroy all that they have; do not spare them, but kill both man and woman, child and infant, ox and sheep, camel and donkey" (1 Sam 15:3)—a frightening statement. And it must be noted that such figures no longer appear in the New Testament. Once again we read about persecuted people, and only the persecuted. The two most important figures in the New Testament, John the Baptist and Jesus, were executed. Their lives, but also the lives of many of their disciples and followers, ended in martyrdom.

It should no longer surprise us to discover that the people the Bible addressed were persecuted too. This applies to the people addressed by the Gospels as well as by 1 Peter and the book of Revelation. After all, persecution was the normal fate of Christians until the fourth century.

The fourth century represents an important turning point in the history of biblical exegesis. After Constantine's conversion, Christians were no longer persecuted; at times they became persecutors themselves. The language of love and trust that had been an integral part of biblical texts in the context of persecution was suddenly transformed into a language of violence and hatred by the new context. The persecuted understand the Bible differently from the persecutors. The powerless interpret it differently from the powerful. When a persecuted Christian praying in the catacombs proclaims God's nearness to his persecuted brothers and sisters and says "God is with us," it is simply quite different from a soldier in an attacking army inscribing "God is with us" on his belt. A frightened Christian making the sign of the cross as a sign of faith in the crucified Lord is quite different from a Roman soldier engraving the cross on his helmet as a sign of the triumphant God. There is a difference between a Jewish survivor of a concentration camp talking of the promise of land and an Israeli settler coming from the United States doing the same.

The Bible, the book of the persecuted, has the crucified Lord as its centerpiece. Only from this center—and with the aid of this hermeneutical key—can the Bible be understood and interpreted correctly.

**6.** Law and Gospel are the hermeneutical keys to interpreting the Bible. Law and Gospel are the two sides of the one righteous God. The God of the Bible is simultaneously the God demanding justice and the God promising it. This becomes clear in the Old Testament when one investigates the words *zadaq* and *shaphat*. The very same word can have different and even contradictory meanings:

> *Zadaq,* "to judge," does not mean to be "impartial" when pronouncing "not guilty" or "guilty." It means instead to resolve a conflict in the interest of the general public in such a way that the person who has been deprived of rights is once again helped to obtain justice, and the disturber of the peace is rendered harmless. Thus a state of the greatest possible public well-being and welfare results.[9]

In the same way, *shaphat* describes action that restores the peace of a community:

> Restitution of the *shalom* is not just viewed from the subject of *shaphat* but also from the object: for the one who suffers under this disturbed order receives *shaphat,* the sound of rescue, of being aided to achieve rights; for the one who caused the disturbance, the action of *shaphat* turns into the excluding and annihilating verdict "guilty." [10]

This is God's righteousness, which becomes apparent in the Old Testament as in the New Testament and which has been revealed in Jesus Christ. Jesus Christ is this righteousness of God, and to that extent Jesus is the center of Scripture. Consequently, whenever we examine a controversy over justice, we must first take a look at the balance of power, for God deals differently with the powerful than with the powerless. God demands justice from the former and promises justice to the latter, which is evident not only in Hannah's song but also in Mary's Magnificat.

The principle of Law and Gospel can readily be applied to the problem of Palestine. On the one hand, we have to pay attention to the balance of power. What is often overlooked is that demands are most often made of Palestinians, even though they are the weak ones, whereas mighty Israel is seldom criticized. More often than not, people even justify Israel's behavior. On the other hand, themes like "election" or "promise of land" must not be considered law or the possession of either side; they must always be seen as promise and gift. Just as God sides with those who stand with empty hands, so do Christians have to be in solidarity with those who are powerless, poor, and oppressed. This is the way in which Martin Luther's teaching on Law and Gospel attains socio-political significance.

In the following chapter I offer some examples of such an interpretation. I encountered these examples in my work during the Intifada, and they mirror our situation, including our fears as well as our faith and hope. It will become apparent that a Protestant theology in the Palestinian context must relate more and more to the Old Testament, and that this theology is of universal rather than merely Palestinian significance, since it is concerned with the center of Scripture.

# CHAPTER 7
# ELECTION

IN THE Old Testament, the verb used for election (*bahar*) first appears as late as the sixth century, although the concept itself is older.[1] Incidentally, that is typical of Holy Scripture. Statements on election did not, after all, fall down from heaven; they are based on experience. First came the experience and only then the designation for it. Israel considered its experience with God to be unique, special, and exclusive. The Old Testament described this experience of a unique relation to God with the term *election*.

"Election" is and will always be a statement of faith; it is solely a promise. It is a promise to those, above all, who see themselves as unworthy, weak, and powerless—to those who begin to despair about themselves. It is to them that God promises election. Thus it is no wonder that most of the statements about election in the Old Testament date from the time of exile. With the exception of the Psalms, most of the statements about election occur in Deuteronomy and Isaiah. A promise is given to the scattered, the defeated, and the banished. We read in Deuteronomy, "It was not because you were more numerous than any other people that the Lord set His heart on you and chose you—for you were the fewest of all the peoples" (Deut 7:7). We see the same thing in Isaiah, the prophet in exile who wrestles with the desperate:

> But Zion said, "The LORD has forsaken me,
>    my Lord has forgotten me."
> Can a woman forget her nursing child,
>    or show no compassion for the child of her womb?
> Even these may forget, yet I will not forget you.
> See, I have inscribed you on the palms of my hands;
>    your walls are continually before me (Isa 49:14–16).

> But you, Israel, my servant, Jacob, whom I have chosen,
>    the offspring of Abraham, my friend;
> you whom I took from the ends of the earth,
>    and called from its farthest corners,
> saying to you, "You are my servant,
>    I have chosen you and not cast you off";
> do not fear, for I am with you,
>    do not be afraid, for I am your God;
> I will strengthen you, I will help you,
>    I will uphold you with my victorious right hand (Isa 41:8–10).

We see this viewpoint in the New Testament also. Jesus, for instance, called those who have been denied their rights the chosen. Accordingly, the result of being chosen is that God will "shortly give them their rights," as Luke 18:7f. tells it in the parable of the widow and the unjust judge. Paul tries to make this understanding of election—which had become visible on the cross—clear to the Corinthians, who had transformed "election" into individualistic fervor:

> Consider your own call, brothers and sisters: not many of you were wise by human standards, not many were powerful, not many were of noble birth. But God chose what is foolish in the world to shame the wise; God chose what is weak in the world to shame the strong; God chose what is low and despised in the world, things that are not, to reduce to nothing things that are, so that no one might boast in the presence of God (1 Cor 1:26–29).

Election, correctly understood, is therefore a promise to the weak, encouragement to the discouraged, and consolation to the desperate.

But election can easily become "claim," and a statement of faith then turn into dangerous ideology. This occurs especially when a person, a religion, or a people becomes strong, secure, or rich. It is alarming to have a promise turn into a claim. That is the time for God to send a prophet, as was the case with the prophet Amos, who appeared when Israel thought itself safe because it was prosperous.

> You only have I known of all the families of the earth;
>    therefore I will punish you for all your iniquities (Amos 3:2; see
>    also Hos 13:4–8).[2]

In a situation such as that, election begins to sound like judgment, punishment, affliction. This understanding of it can also be found in the New Testament. In order to prevent faith in election from turning into a claim, Jesus ended several of his parables with the assertion, "For many are called, but few are chosen" (Matt 22:14).

Election is not a special privilege. It is much more a call to service, above all a service "to the other." The election of Israel did not occur for its own sake. Israel was chosen in order to turn its people into witnesses to the pagans, so that they too might participate in election. Election was already meant to include rather than exclude the whole world in the Old Testament. This is expressed particularly in Isaiah:

> I am the LORD, I have called you in righteousness,
>     I have taken you by the hand and kept you;
> I have given you as a covenant to the people,
>     a light to the nations (Isa 42:6; see also Isa 55:4–5).

At the beginning of the Torah and the whole Holy Scripture stands a promise from God that is to be taken seriously, namely, that "all families of the earth shall be blessed" (Gen 12:3) through Abraham's call.

Election is and will always be God's action alone, which a human can never make exclusively his or her own, but which can be gambled away. Election by God is not "an eternal unchangeable decree" to which God "would be subject once and for all."[3] Election should instead really be interpreted, proclaimed, and actualized again and again, depending on the context (see 2 Cor 17:20; 21:14; Hos 1:9; 13:1; Jer 31:31–34).

Consequently election results in praise of God, responsibility before the world and before fellow humans. We encounter this interpretation in Romans 9–11, and we should take a closer look at the summary form of these three important chapters by the Apostle Paul.

## Romans 9–11

The problem Paul addresses in Romans 9–11[4] is that even though Israel possesses filiation, glory, covenants, enactment of laws, worship, promises, and the patriarchs, it does not accept God's promise in Christ (Rom 9:1–5).

This allows Paul to raise the question whether God's Word has failed, that is, whether it has lost its power (Rom 9:6a). He refutes this possibility, however, on the grounds that already in the Old Testament election was always and solely based on the freedom of God, and was never transmittable genealogically. That is how it was with Abraham, with Isaac, and with Jacob. Their election depended solely on the call from God. Paul refers to the Torah and turns it against Israel's claim to election, carrying its claim to the absurd. Since election is nothing but grace, no human being, not even Israel, can assert its rights before God. Yet whoever opposes the call of God (Pharaoh, for example) is driven back into his or her limitations by God (Rom 9:14–18). In view of the fundamental difference between God the Creator and human creatures, the latter are well advised not to argue with God (Rom 9:19–21). This also applies to present experience, when—through God's call in the Gospel—God transforms the pagans into God's own people in accordance with the promise in the Old Testament (Hos 2:13). Yet a remnant of Israel will be rescued in accordance with God's promise in Isaiah (Isa 10:22; 1:9), and that, too, is God's doing (Rom 9:22–29). "What then are we to say? Gentiles who did not strive for righteousness have attained it, that is, righteousness through faith. But Israel, who did strive for the righteousness that is based on the law, did not succeed in fulfilling that law" (Rom 9:30–31).

Israel failed because it laid claim to election as law, according to Paul. But Christ has put an end to all law (Rom 10:4). In him the law has achieved its real purpose and election its original meaning. Henceforth Christ is God's consolation to everyone who has faith, Jew or Gentile (Rom 10:5–13). Christ is revealed as God's consolation in proclamation. But Paul discovered that a large number of Jews did not believe in this proclamation (Rom 10:14–21).

Did God then reject God's people? Far from it! (Rom 11:1). Paul and the first disciples and Christian communities were, after all, themselves Jews who had come to believe in Christ. They constituted a holy remnant who considered themselves the elect, but only by grace. One can see that God did not reject God's people by the fact that there were Jewish Christians and there are still messianic Christians (Rom 11:1–10). But because the rest of the Jews stumbled, salvation reached the Gentiles (Rom 11:11–16).

But this does not mean that Gentile Christians should feel superior to the Jews who did not achieve faith in Christ, for then they would turn their election into a claim and thus gamble it away. They must remember that they have been cut from the wild olive tree and grafted unto a cultivated olive tree after some branches had been chopped off that cultivated tree. But how should this image be interpreted? I agree with Nicholas Walter, who writes:

> In my opinion, Israel is not the olive tree or the trunk, and certainly not the root, despite Jeremiah 11:16, for "Israel" is the branches of the olive—which have now—due to their non-acceptance of Jesus Christ—been in large measure removed (Rom 11:25b). Nor are the Gentiles the wild tree. Instead, the believers among the Gentiles are the newly grafted branches which have been removed from the "natural" wild tree, paganism. In my opinion, if one were to interpret the cultivated olive tree, its roots and the sap that flows into its branches and fruit, one would probably point first to God—to God's electing and promising, and the saving grace streaming from Him—but not identify it immediately with Israel. The election of the Gentiles should consequently be understood as a promise that has its roots and foundation solely in God's faithfulness (Rom 11:17–24).[5]

Yet one cannot set limits on God's faithfulness, nor on Israel's unbelief. Paul can express this only by means of a mystery: "A hardening has come upon part of Israel, until the full number of the Gentiles has come in" (Rom 11:25). And so all Israel will be saved in this way. Anyone who experiences God's promise as justification of the godless cannot limit God's election to him- or herself. All are included *in spe* and *sub contraria specie*. Paul gives a Christological explanation for the salvation of "all Israel." The mystery does not deal with any speculation about the future but rather with a statement of faith about the God who justifies the godless, raises the dead, and calls into being what is not. That is why Paul ends his explanations with the profound sentence "For God has imprisoned all in disobedience so that he may be merciful to all" (Rom 11:32).

Election, understood as promise, surpasses all reason and perception and results in one's joining in praise of the God "from whom, through whom, and to whom are all things." To God alone, then, is due the glory forever (Rom 11:33–36).

## Election Today?

The phenomenon of an individual, group, or people viewing its relationship to God as unique and believing itself to be the chosen, is one shared by all monotheistic religions. Pious Jews believe that they, or rather their people, are the chosen people. Pious Christians, on the other hand, believe that they have become the chosen people through Christ. Muslims have similar beliefs. This phenomenon is probably connected to one's "direct impression of one's 'own' God," who, "in His stepping forward as 'the one' God—ground and limit of all being, meaning and joy of all existence, and possibility and future of all true life," can be experienced as "effective."[6]

It is natural and understandable that Israel should consider its history with God to be unique. One should respect and honor it as an expression of faith, but one need not consider it to be objective truth. The structures of faith are very like the structures of love. Just as a lover cannot help but see his or her beloved as "the one" special one, and the "lily among the flowers," so a believer cannot do other than view his or her connectedness to God as unique and exclusive.

If this statement of faith is objectified or even absolutized by any particular group, it loses its rightful setting in life (*Sitz im Leben*) and is transformed into a dangerous ideology. There is only a small difference between faith and ideology, but it is a real one. As a Christian, I have no choice but to believe that without any effort on my part God has chosen me through Christ. But this does not mean that I must immediately declare "the others" not chosen. Nor can I invent any kind of objective theological dogma about the continuing election of the Jewish people or anyone else. We human beings in this world have no business to determine who is or who is not chosen. Separating them is an eschatological matter and is God's business alone (see the parable about the weeds among the wheat in Matt 13:24–30). This separation cuts right through our own house, so we are warned never to raise election into a claim. If, as a Christian, I meet a Jew who believes in the election of his people, I am able not only to respect his belief but also to take it seriously with appropriate awe and to share his hope of God's promise. Yet as a Christian, I cannot stop praying for him and testifying to him my faith in Christ who, I believe, is God's election for all (and therefore for him too).

God's election applied in the Old Testament already to a people but not to a particular state. The Old Testament distinguishes between them but does not separate them, for the interpretation of election bore consequences for the political life, indeed the very survival, of Israel. Its future always depended—especially whenever it was in control of a state—on whether it understood its election as law or as promise, which most often became evident by the way it handled the power available to it. Did it rely on its own power or on God's, and did it exercise its power on behalf of the poor and the weak or on behalf of the strong and the rich?

Today's Judaism is once again faced with the challenge of seeing and interpreting the concept of election in biblical terms. "Judaism must reject the dogma of election insofar as it does not mean serving and being different but instead means being superior"[7] is the justified declaration of the Israeli theologian Talmon. The thought of election linked to a belief in superiority is a dangerous ideology that results in isolation (see, for example, how, in Ps 78:67–70, Judah cheered the destruction of the Northern Kingdom and denied them election). Throughout history, election—misunderstood and falsely practiced—has resulted in crusades, racism, apartheid, and Nazism.

Unfortunately, one cannot avoid the impression that the state of Israel equates its being chosen with being superior, a superiority that was—or rather, is—related to colonialist and imperialist claims to power. Many immigrant Jews at the end of the last century and the beginning of this century displayed this arrogance and attitude of superiority and acted like colonialists toward the native inhabitants, even though Palestine had been a land of culture long before Europe even had an inkling of civilization. Looking at the state of Israel today, one wonders whether Israel's election perhaps consists of getting away with things not permitted to other states in the region. It is the only state in the region possessing nuclear weapons; it is the only state in the world allowed to ignore United Nations resolutions; it is the only state to behave like America's pet, obtaining sympathy, access to the media, and access to huge amounts of economic and military aid. Can this be the sign of today's election of Israel? Or is it not, rather, abuse of power on the part of Israel, made possible by the support of the great powers, which could prove to be harmful to Israel's future as well?

The decisive question posed to Israel also concerns Palestinians: how will Israel handle the power available to it? Will it use it to dominate Palestinians or to liberate them and itself? The answer to the question will determine whether a second South Africa is created—or rather, continued—in Israel/Palestine, or whether a democratic oasis is established there. The answer will also determine whether Israel understands its election as claim or as promise.

Israel's election forces us to reflect on God's relationship to peoples. The fact that God dealt with Israel in the Old Testament should not tempt us to think that God dealt only with Israel. God has not ceased to be Creator and Preserver of the whole world. The fact that we have only the record of Israel's experiences with God in the Bible does not mean that God had no interest in other peoples. The Old Testament itself confirms this in the book of Jonah, when the prophet speaks to those Israelites who "out of their particular existence made demands before God which impinge on Yahweh's freedom to make plans with other peoples," with the goal of making clear to them that Yahweh's plans encompass all the peoples of the world. God felt sorry for Nineveh, its inhabitants, yes, even the animals there (Jonah 4:11) even though Nineveh was the capital of the Assyrian Empire, Israel's greatest enemy. The prophet Amos demonstrates clearly that God treated even Israel's enemies with grace:

> Are you not like the Ethiopians to me,
>     O people of Israel? says the LORD.
> Did I not bring Israel up from the land of Egypt,
>     and the Philistines from Caphtor and Arameans from Kir?
> (Amos 9:7)

Amos shows that the Exodus was not a unique rescue involving Israel only. God also dealt with Israel's hostile neighbors and shared "exoduses" with them.

Thus faith in the election of Israel and the liberation of Palestinians need not contradict each other, for "the God of Israel" is also interested in the Palestinians and in their welfare. The faith of the God of Israel who is not indifferent to Israel's neighboring peoples could eventually become a theological reason for the cooperation of all states existing in the Middle East. Since God is not indifferent to these other peoples, Israel has the duty to be a light to them also (Isa 42:6), to let them share in the blessing of Abraham (Gen 12:2f.) so that "a people of the God of Abraham" (Ps 47:9) rises out of Israel and these peoples. In the Old Testament the concept of "people of the God of Abraham" increasingly became the subject of hope. We Christians believe that it became a reality through Christ. And Muslims too understand themselves to be descendants of Abraham.

Wouldn't it be theologically possible for Jews, Christians, and Muslims —especially in the Middle East—to remember their common roots as well as their future in the patriarch of the faith, Abraham, and so urge their people to respect and cooperate with each other in order to share in the blessing of Abraham?

# CHAPTER 8

# THE PROMISE OF LAND

PARTICULAR PASSAGES in the Old Testament referring to "promises of land" are often cited in support of the modern state of Israel and its policy of occupying the West Bank and the Gaza Strip—not only by rightist politicians like Yitzhak Shamir or radical right-wing groups like Gush Emunim, but also by ordinary Christians and some Christian theologians. Many people think that the link between the biblical promise of land and the modern state of Israel is a plausible one and could be reestablished. But after careful examination, it becomes evident that this link—historically naive—is theologically questionable and not so simple to reestablish on biblical grounds.

It is not so easy to apply the promises of land to the present state of Israel and the occupied territories, because the biblical evidence is ambivalent. How are the boundaries of the promised land drawn? If one studies the texts, one finds that God did not draw an unequivocal map. On the contrary, the boundaries of the promised land vary greatly, depending on the author, the time of writing, and the circumstances.[1]

In Genesis 15:18, for example, the "river of Egypt" (which probably refers to the Arish Wadi between Gaza and the eastern border of the Nile delta) in the south and the Euphrates River in the north are named as boundaries. The eastern border is not specified. The borders named here are in accord with the extent of Solomon's empire at the time of its greatest expanse (1 Kings 4:24).

The borders are described in greater detail in the book of Numbers (34:2–13): the southern border runs from the Mediterranean Sea and the "wadi of Egypt" through the wilderness of Zin to the southern end of the Dead Sea. The northern border runs from the Mediterranean at Mount Hor to Hazar-Enan, encompassing the territory of present-day Lebanon. The eastern border included present-day Damascus and a large part of Jordan.

These borders, however, never did reflect reality; rather, they represent later visions. Not even the borders named in connection with the conquered lands (see Josh 13:19) or those from Dan in the north to Beersheba in the south are historically accurate, as can be clearly seen when one looks at Judges 1.

So what does this finding have to do with citing the promise of land today? Should the present state of Israel appeal to the borders of the empire of David and Solomon (which lasted only 40 years), or to those established by Joshua, or to those of the Northern Kingdom or of Judah? Should Israel go to war in order to occupy Sinai, Lebanon, parts of Syria and Iraq and so help fulfill the promise? Or should Israel continue to exist without an accepted constitution and without a border guaranteed by international law? As Hans Küng has written:

> In the matter of borders, one must distinguish between divine revelation and national ideology. No Jew is obligated to defend borders that may have been more or less established by God. The Bible has given Jews in Israel the freedom to come to a rational understanding with their neighbors.[2]

Cannot the fact that the biblical borders are variable help the Israel of today to be satisfied with the territory set in 1948 and to withdraw from the occupied territories? Could they not win peace instead of a war?

There never was a purely Jewish state, not even in biblical times. The Bible is quite realistic on that point. But this constitutes a basic difference between the Old Testament and modern Zionist literature. "The land without people" for "the people without land" cannot be found in the Old Testament; it is a modern myth. The Old Testament does not hide the fact that other peoples have always lived in the promised land. Abraham, for example, wandered around Canaan as a stranger without property. Genesis relates how Hebron belonged to the Hittites and how Abraham was forced to purchase a burying place for himself and his wife and children (Gen 23:1–20).

According to the story of the conquest of land in Joshua and in Judges, Israelite and non-Israelite tribes and peoples lived as neighbors in Canaan both during and after the conquest. We read about the tribe of Benjamin, for example, "But the Benjaminites did not drive out the Jebusites who lived in Jerusalem; so the Jebusites have lived in Jerusalem among the Benjaminites to this day" (Judges 1:21).

A pure Jewish state did not exist at the beginning; it did not exist after the conquests of land; the Bible did not envision its existence in the future either. Jeremiah, for example, said that the peoples should dwell in the midst of Israel (Jer 12:16). The prophets established the peoples' close connection to the land through their description of the pilgrimages of the peoples to Zion (Isa 2:2–5).

We Christians believe that the end-time has already begun with the coming of Jesus of Nazareth and the sending of the Holy Spirit. During the end-time all the peoples will convert to the one God and will make pilgrimages to Zion. "The peoples will no longer be strangers and aliens in Israel, they will be citizens with the saints and also members of the household of God. (See Eph 2:19.) His house is the land."[3] Believers in Christ receive a share of this gift too. The presence of Christians in the "promised land" is the fulfillment of one of the divine promises too. There is absolutely no doubt that they belong here.

The Pentateuch, specifically Deuteronomy, reveals the following picture of the promise of land, conquest of land, and loss of land: the promise of land made to the patriarchs, the time of Moses, and the wilderness generation was fulfilled completely by the conquest of it under Joshua:

> Thus the LORD gave to Israel all the land that he swore to their ancestors that he would give them; and having taken possession of it, they settled there. And the LORD gave them rest on every side just as he had sworn to their ancestors; not one of all their enemies had withstood them, for the LORD had given all their enemies into their hands. Not one of all the good promises that the LORD had made to the house of Israel had failed; all came to pass (Jos 21:43–45).

But taking possession of the land was tied to obedience to God. That is why Moses, Aaron (Num 20:12), and the wilderness generation (Deut 1:35) were denied entrance into the promised land. Caleb was the only member of that generation allowed to see the land (Deut 1:35f.), only because he had "wholeheartedly" followed God (Jos 14:6). But it is very interesting to note that Caleb was not by ancestry an Israelite stemming from the house of Jacob, but rather an Edomite, or Kenizzite, a descendant of Esau (Gen 36:11 and 15), who had probably joined the tribe of Judah (1 Chron 4:13). It is he who was heir to the promised land and was given Hebron and its vicinity in the south of Judah (Jos 14:6–15).

Living on the land and keeping it was just as much tied to obedience to God as taking possession of it. God announced through Moses that should Israel become disobedient it would lose the land (Lev 26:31–39; Deut 4:25–28; 28:63–68). Fulfillment of this threat was demonstrated by the fall of Samaria through the Assyrians in 722 and the destruction of Jerusalem by the Babylonians in 587 because of Israel's disobedience (1 Kings 17:7–23; 21:10–16; 23:26f.; 24:3f.) Two things are stressed in this connection: violation of the First Commandment and the shedding of innocent blood. Thus God's commandments and human rights are here seen as interrelated (see also Ezek 33:21–26). That is the way Israel's obedience or disobedience is made evident. Obedience remained the condition for a repossession of the land (Lev 26:39–45; Deut 30:1–10).

It is interesting to note that most of the promises of land in the Bible stem from the time of the patriarchs or from the time of the exile (especially the Deuteronomist or the Priestly source and the exilic prophets) and thus from a time when Israel actually had no land of its own. As a matter of fact, these promises were meant to be promises and words of hope to a people who were weak and stateless. That is why the fulfillment of the promises was called a miracle and the act of God himself. That is the rightful setting in life of these promises.

But in situations when Israel had control over a state, a territory, and an army, God's word came instead to admonish Israel to do justice. As far as God was concerned, land without justice was out of the question, and that applied to Israel as well. The aspect of claim was stressed in this connection: possession of land should never be turned into a claim (Amos 2:13–16; Isa 28:21; 29:1ff.; Jer 21:4ff.), not even after the return from Babylonian captivity (Mal 3:24). Here too the principle is valid: "The land is mine; with me you are but aliens and tenants" (Lev 25:23).

This observation is important, for if the Jews driven out of Europe and the Holocaust survivors saw a fulfillment of the Old Testament promise of land in their own immigration to Palestine, this should be honored and respected as a testimony and expression of their faith. But today after the Palestinian Intifada, one must be clear about what it means to persist in talking about the promise of land and its fulfillment in the state of Israel. In Israel today, public reference to the promise of land is used by radical fundamentalist groups to justify continued occupation of the West Bank and Gaza. That is how the policy of settlement on Palestinian soil is explained and the taking of land is justified.

The Old Testament indeed mentions a promise of land, but nowhere is a real, existing state viewed as the bearer of that promise. On the contrary, Holy Scripture is very skeptical about the establishment of states. The Bible considers Israel's desire to have its own king "like all the other nations" a rejection of God (1 Sam 8:5–8). Samuel receives the command to warn them and "show them the ways of the king":

> He will take your sons and appoint them to his chariots and to be his horsemen, and to run before his chariots; and he will appoint for himself commanders of thousands and commanders of fifties, and some to plow his ground and to reap his harvest, and to make his implements of war and the equipment of his chariots. He will take your daughters to be perfumers and cooks and bakers. He will take the best of your fields and vineyards and olive orchards and give them to his courtiers. He will take one-tenth of your grain and of your vineyards and give it to his officers and his courtiers. He will take your male and female slaves, and the best of your cattle and donkeys, and put them to his work. He will take one-tenth of your flocks, and you shall be his slaves. (1 Sam 8:11–17; see also 1 Sam 10 and 12).

Yet the Bible acknowledges the necessity of having a state, especially considering the constant threat from the Philistines (1 Sam 9:16). But it insists on an essential difference between the king of Israel and the kings of other nations. The king of Israel is subject to the law of God; obedience is demanded from him, and justice is expected. He is repeatedly warned against relying solely on power, on army and weapons (Deut 17:14–20; 2 Sam 23:3; Ps 33:16–18; 147:10f.) The prophets are assigned the duty of watching over him (1 Sam 15; 2 Sam 12:24f.; 2 Kings 1). Individual kings were rated according to their obedience to these laws.

Skepticism toward monarchy, bad experiences with many of the ruling kings, and deep disappointments with them, along with the exile occurring during this time finally resulted in an eschatological interpretation of "monarchy." Messianic expectations began to appear. This is when the idea emerges of a coming ruler who will rule justly and wisely and in whose time there will be "peace without end" (Isa 9:5f.; 11:1–10; Micah 5:1–5; Jer 23:5f.; Zech 9:9f.). The idea of "Messiah" expands the narrow national concepts of "king." "Peace" is increasingly interpreted to mean Israel's peace with its neighbors and is even expanded to encompass the whole world. It is no longer viewed as peace for Israel at the expense of others.

At this point the New Testament links up with the Old Testament. Scripture links neither the Messiah nor God's kingdom to any existing or future earthly kingdom or state. In my opinion, this was not just determined by history; it was theologically necessary, for this was how skepticism toward every institution of a worldly state was maintained, an exclusive nationalism was blown out of existence, and justice and freedom achieved universal significance.

Holy Scripture is much more cautious in its statements than many modern ecclesiastical statements that see "a sign of God's faithfulness"[4] in the founding of the state of Israel in 1948. No substantiation can be found in either the Old Testament or the New Testament for such a viewpoint. That kind of talk gives up biblical skepticism, and thus one comes close to a nationalistic religious ideology. Then one loses the insight that the most beautiful words regarding God's faithfulness to God's people most frequently—and certainly not coincidentally—stem from the time of exile. Something else is also ignored in such talk:

> In the course of their history, the Jewish people, too, experienced—not without God's providence—revolutionary changes in their circumstances. They existed with a state as well as without a state; they lived with these borders, as well as with those borders. And the Jewish people could very easily—speaking hypothetically—live once again without a state, with these or with other borders. Throughout history, God's chosen "people" and the promised "land" have belonged to the "essence" of Judaism as religion, but not to a concrete form of organization (state) with definite borders—no matter how self-evidently, under present conditions, Judaism as a people has the right to a state of its own.[5]

To see the fulfillment of a divine promise in the existing state of Israel is, therefore, neither biblical nor theologically accurate. Yet today's state of Israel is a political necessity, given the history of the nineteenth and twentieth centuries. If this more or less secular state wishes to be respected, it must comply with international law and allow itself to be measured by it. Its ties to Judaism cannot free it from this duty. Rather, these ties increase its obligation.

Many Western Christian theologians, by emphasizing the continuity from the Old Testament Israel to today's state of Israel, tried very hard to work out and give reasons for the validity of the promise of land to the modern state of Israel. The aim of these efforts was, above all, to counteract the thesis that Judaism is merely a religion, to understand that Jews are a people, and to learn that a land of their own is of great importance to their existence—a totally understandable aim after 1945!

The cynical aspect of the story is, however, that precisely those theologians who tried to counteract the spiritualization of Judaism (into a religion) and of the promise of land (into eternal life), either knowingly or unknowingly fell into the trap of spiritualizing the land in another way. They referred to the land—one must describe it more specifically as "the land of Palestine"—in the same way that the Zionists had at the beginning of the century, as a land without a native people. They ignored the fact that Palestine was not an unpopulated space, that it had not remained a fallow land, and that a people with a two-thousand-year history lived on this land.

That the promise of land for Israel meant the expropriation of Palestinians' land was not considered a theological problem. Only here and there did someone notice that human rights were being violated in the name of "divine rights."

At the same time that one considered the founding of the state of Israel to be the fulfillment of the divine promise, one also considered Israel's expropriation of Palestine and the expulsion of about one million Palestinians to be a purely human problem. Although Christian believers throughout the whole world were emotionally moved by the interpretation declaring that Israel was founded by divine will, the expulsion of Palestinians touched only their purses (for example, the establishment of the Department of Service to Palestinian Refugees of the World Council of Churches and Middle East Council of Churches). Dogmatics and ethics had become separated; God and humans no longer had anything to do with each other.

The God of Holy Scripture is the God of history—and this is how God is distinguished from "false gods." In faith, history is taken very seriously, and biblical faith is included in the movement of history, which is how it keeps its essence as faith and avoids becoming an inflexible ideology tinted with religiosity.

It is this characteristic of biblical faith that is lost in fundamentalism—Jewish, Christian, or Muslim. To fundamentalists, the ideal, the yearned for, and the longingly awaited future is nothing but a specific era of the past. The book of Revelation, for example, is a description of the future to Christian fundamentalists. Muslim fundamentalists, on the other hand, want to reinstate the time of the Caliph Omar—with all that this implies. Jewish fundamentalists also attempt to transfer themselves back to a specific Old Testament period. The ties of the texts to history, their very rootedness in history, are overlooked and even denied.

A certain fundamentalist way of speaking about the promise of land is very dangerous because it ignores history. Thoroughgoing fundamentalists do not stop with the Old Testament promise of land. They demand much more, such as, for instance:

> rebuilding the temple, reintroducing animal sacrifice, official toleration of slavery, the death penalty for certain transgressions of ritual laws, and restitution of a theocratic state under a high priest. As though the rest of God's history with his people, which was in large measure unconnected to a "state," did not have religious significance. As though it could be God's will to strive to restitute some status quo of long ago.[6]

Just how dangerous this way of looking at things is can be seen in the activities of the Jewish radical rightists, Ateret Kohanim, who attempt to settle in the Christian and Muslim districts of Jerusalem's Old City with the aim of destroying the Dome on the Rock at some future date so as to found a new temple in its place.

Thus one can state: Every thesis that still clings to an exclusive "Greater Israel" or "Greater Palestine" should be rejected as a fanatic and extreme ideology. Like it or not, the fact is that there are two peoples living in the geographic territory of Palestine, and their fates can no longer be separated. For God's sake, for the sake of humanity, and for their own sake, Israel must not cling to a Greater Israel. An Israeli claim to all of Palestine is impossible on the basis of either ancient or modern history. Meanwhile, a large number of Palestinians have declared their readiness to share the land with the Israelis, so that the Jewish people persecuted by the whole world can have a homeland.

The land happens to be the homeland of two peoples. Each of them should understand this land to be a gift of God to be shared with the other. Peace and the blessing on the land and on the two peoples will depend on this sharing. Only then will the biblical promises be fulfilled.

# CHAPTER 9

# THE EXODUS

THE BOOK of Exodus plays a particular role in the Bible and its interpretation history. Just as the Pentateuch (the five books of Moses) constitutes the center of the Old Testament, so is Exodus the heart of the Pentateuch. Thus one can label it the most holy book in the Hebrew Bible. The center of the book is the event of the Hebrews being led out of Egypt, which is called simply Yahweh's event. But this event never was considered merely a part of past history. It was always a part of the present and the future as well.

The Old Testament prophets repeatedly took up the Exodus event and pictured it as present reality for their listeners. Sometimes it was interpreted as a call to judgment but at other times as promise. Whether recalling this founding date of Israel's history was used as warning or promise always depended on Israel's circumstances at the time. The Exodus was never recalled out of context. It was never a timeless and mechanistic principle but always concrete.

The book of the prophet Hosea is a good example. Hosea was active from approximately 755 to 724 B.C.E., which allowed him to experience several phases of Israel's history. In 733/2, Israel experienced an economic upswing. The Israelites enjoyed prosperity as well as the military strength of a superpower. But this was blasphemy to Hosea, so the prophet stood up and announced the coming trial as a return to Egypt:

> Do not rejoice, O Israel
>   Do not exult as other nations do;
> for you have played the whore, departing from your God.
>   You have loved a prostitute's pay
>   on all the threshing floors.
> Threshing floor and wine vat shall not feed them,

> and the new wine shall fail them.
> They shall not remain in the land of the LORD;
>> but Ephraim shall return to Egypt,
>> and in Assyria they shall eat unclean food
> (Hosea 9:1–3; see also 11:5).

Separation from God results in separation from land (Hosea 9:15). According to the prophet, the Exodus can be reversed and revoked.

But the prophet spoke very differently just eight years later. Assyria had besieged Samaria in 724, a totally new situation for Israel. The prophet at this point brought up the Exodus tradition again, but this time in a very different tone. He announced to besieged Israel that a new exodus would surpass the old one:

> They shall come trembling like birds from Egypt,
>> and like doves from the land of Assyria;
>> and I will return to their homes, says the LORD (Hosea 11:11).

The Exodus, in this new context, became a promise. The same thing can be seen with other prophets. The prophet Amos appeared in the days of Jeroboam II, one of the times Israel was prospering, but at a cost of great social losses. Amos referred to the Exodus and drew a parallel:

> Are you not like the Ethiopians to me,
>> O people of Israel? says the LORD.
> Did I not bring Israel up from the land of Egypt,
>> and the Philistines from Caphtor
>> and the Arameans from Kir? (Amos 9:7).

The moment one derives a claim from the Exodus, it loses its rightful setting and thus its meaning. Because Israel had abused the Exodus by using it to its own advantage, the prophet Amos used the Exodus to pronounce a judgment on Israel and to urge it to assume responsibility. In a situation like that, "bringing home" can turn into an affliction:

> You only have I known
>> of all the families of the earth;
> therefore I will punish you
>> for all your iniquities (Amos 3:2).

Yet how differently Isaiah speaks from exile! To the people driven out of Babylon he promises liberation from this foreign rule, a new exodus:

> But now thus says the LORD,
>> he who created you, O Jacob,
>> he who formed you, O Israel:
> Do not fear, for I have redeemed you;
>> I have called you by name, you are mine.
> When you pass through the waters, I will be with you;
>> and through the rivers, they shall not overwhelm you;
> when you walk though the fire you shall not be burned,
>> and the flame shall not consume you.
> For I am the LORD your God,
>> the Holy One of Israel, your Savior.
> I give Egypt as your ransom,
>> Ethiopia and Seba in exchange for you.
> Because you are precious in my sight,
>> and honored, and I love you,
> I give people in return for you,
>> nations in exchange for your life.
> Do not fear, for I am with you;
>> I will bring your offspring from the east,
>> and from the west I will gather you;
> I will say to the north, "Give them up,"
>> and to the south, "Do not withhold;
> bring my sons from far away
>> and my daughters from the end of the earth—" (Isa 43:1–6)

The history of the effects of the Exodus becomes evident from these examples. One can also observe how important it was to the prophets to take into account the context of their listeners in every interpretation they made. It was from the context that the prophets determined whether they would apply the Exodus story as judgment, warning, or promise.

If the Jews saw their liberation from Hitler's yoke and their rescue from the Holocaust as a new exodus, that should be accepted as an expression of their faith in the God of liberators. In these circumstances, when Jews were without power, without land, and without a state, the Exodus was a promise. But the Jews, once deprived of power in Europe, have become powerful. They have founded a state of their own in a land that had been inhabited by another people for thousands of years. One should now reproach them with the Exodus, warning them not to forget their time "in Egypt" and exhorting them not to assume the role of Pharaoh themselves. Experiencing the Exodus is not a permanent guarantee. Just as God entrusted the Torah to the people liberated out of Egypt, so should Israel uphold human rights in its dealings with the Palestinians. There is no exodus without justice in the Bible.

The New Testament, too, contains citations from the Exodus story, or rather from various aspects of the Exodus tradition in relation to the context of those addressed. The various New Testament authors point to those Exodus stories they think reflect the circumstances of those they are addressing. These authors employ the Exodus tradition as a "type," an example relevant to the present. Paul wrote to the Corinthians, "These things happened to them to serve as an example, and they were written down to instruct us, on whom the ends of the ages have come" (1 Cor 10:11).

Paul sees the time of the wilderness generation reflected in the Corinthian community (1 Cor 10:1–13). There is a parallel, for just as all in the wilderness generation had a share in the special gifts, so too did the Corinthian believers share in the gifts of the sacraments and the Spirit. This participation in the Spirit moved the Corinthian community to enthusiasm, leading to libertinism. Unlimited freedom was practiced in matters of sex. They took part unreservedly in meals from pagan sacrifices. This Christian congregation was in danger of falling into the same critical situation as the people liberated from Egypt. The Exodus stories were therefore a warning to the Christians in this situation. Just as the Exodus from Egypt (including the preservation of the people in the wilderness) did not guarantee entrance into the promised land, so did the sacraments not offer automatic salvation. Paul therefore reminded the Corinthians of the fate of those liberated by the Exodus in order to warn them against lust, idolatry, fornication, and grumbling, for what counts is to go on resisting temptation and fighting sin.

The basic facts of the Exodus serve as a model for the author of the Letter to the Hebrews as well (Heb 11:1–12:3). Although we are not fully acquainted with the circumstances of the people this letter addressed, it is clear they were already being persecuted and that these persecutions strongly challenged their patience and confidence (Heb 10:32ff.). I suspect that they were being persecuted by the state authorities, thus suffering many other handicaps as well. The author of Hebrews was concerned to point to those Exodus stories that would highlight the conflict between the state powers and the people. The author therefore cited those stories in Exodus that parallel the circumstances of the people to whom he is writing. Moses is introduced as a model for the Christian community. He too had been exposed to Pharaoh's persecution. But he did not run away from it. Instead, he "persevered as though he saw him who is invisible" (Heb 11:27). He was even prepared to take handicaps in stride, "for he was looking ahead to the reward" (Heb 11:26). Moses could accomplish all this only "by faith." That is why the Christian community should draw strength and patience from the example of Moses, so they could survive the battle. Because everything depends so much on faith, the congregation should look "to Jesus the pioneer and perfector of our faith, who for the sake of the joy that was set before him endured the cross, disregarding its shame" (Heb 12:2). The congregation should consider this so that they not "grow weary and lose heart" (Heb 12:3).

Stephen, in defending himself before the council, also refers to Moses and the Exodus (Acts 7). Luke wrote Acts under different circumstances from those existing at the time of the Letter to the Hebrews, so Stephen told Exodus stories differently (Acts 7:11ff.). Luke's addressees also suffered persecution, but they were being persecuted by the Jewish communities rather than by state authorities. What bothers the author and his readers is undoubtedly the fact that the majority of the Jews opposed and rejected the message of the Christian missionaries, even though these missionaries had turned first to the Jews and preached in their synagogues. The Jews even went so far as to bring charges against the Christians before the secular courts (Acts 17:7). The secular authorities could no longer ignore the situation in the face of these charges. They were forced at least to investigate them.

Luke's attitude toward the Roman authorities is remarkably favorable. The state representatives all certify Paul's innocence (for example, Acts 23:29; 24:24; 25:18f.; 26:31–33). The Exodus stories he cites reflect this situation. Only one verse refers to Pharaoh's oppression of the Hebrews. And, in this connection, Acts even stated specifically that this applied to "another king who had not known Joseph" (Acts 7:18). There is even some favorable light shed on Pharaoh, since his daughter took Moses in and raised him "as her son." What matters to Luke in the stories he cites is to show how much lack of understanding, denial, and opposition Moses met with—not from the Egyptians but from the Hebrews.

The fate of the Christian missionaries was like that of Moses. The Israelites persecuted their prophets and their saviors too. Thus Stephen's rebuke at the end of his speech is not coincidental:

> You stiff-necked people, uncircumcised in heart and ears, you are forever opposing the Holy Spirit just as your ancestors used to do. Which of the prophets did your ancestors not persecute? They killed those who foretold the coming of the Righteous One, and now you have become his betrayers and murderers (Acts 7:51–52).

Whereas Stephen's comparison to the Exodus has an accusatory tone, charging the people with persecuting even their savior, Matthew's reference to the Exodus is different. It is not the people but the rulers who persecuted both Moses and Jesus in their childhoods. For Matthew, "If Herod's typological model is Pharaoh, then the child Jesus is Moses as a child."[1] But just as Moses is rescued from Pharaoh's hold, so does God protect God's son from all danger. By referring to the Exodus in this way, the Evangelist succeeds in giving the Gospel of Jesus Christ a new interpretation to his Jewish readers. It becomes evident that in Jesus:

> the move out of Egypt is repeated and completed. . . . Matthew's thought is probably "Salvation recurs once again." The reader well acquainted with the Bible senses that God's action in His Son has a fundamental character, linking it to Israel's basic experience and completing it anew.[2]

The Exodus released a totally different history of effects in so-called liberation theology, by attaining a new significance for the oppressed people of Latin America in their struggle for justice. They realized that the political and social suppression they suffered was evil—thus also and precisely a sin against God. They recognized the God of the Exodus as the liberator who identifies closely with them and frees them physically, psychologically, and spiritually from oppression. The church is commanded to participate in the fight for liberation. It is no wonder that the book of Exodus plays a decisive role in this theology, and why it is called liberation theology.

But how can a Palestinian read the book of Exodus? If the book is given a typological exegesis, it loses its socio-political meaning. Yet if it is understood historically, it creates a problem for the Palestinians, for leading the Hebrews out of Egypt is the precondition for taking the land of Palestine. If the Exodus of the Hebrews brought an end to foreign oppression and the attainment of a land of their own, then it meant exactly the opposite to the original inhabitants of Palestine, namely the invasion of their own soil and being dispossessed by foreign troops. After the Jews labeled their "occupation" of Palestine in the 1930s and '40s an "Exodus," the Palestinians had even greater difficulty understanding the book of Exodus. The flip side of the rescue of persecuted Jews is that it spells tragedy for the Palestinian people.

Is there a way out of this dilemma? Can the Palestinians find another way to interpret this book? I was faced with this dilemma when I was about to prepare for a class in religion on the subject of the Exodus. After much indecision, I decided simply to recount the story the way we knew it in the Bible and the way it can be read in every history of Israel. I used the method of interpretation the Old Testament prophets had used, as well as the New Testament evangelists and the liberation theologians. I recounted the story to my young students in this way:

> About 3000 years ago, there was a small Bedouin tribe living in Canaan. Their members were wandering shepherds, who set up their tents wherever there was water and pasture at hand. But the rains failed one year. The land became too dry to provide grazing, and the animals were starving. The shepherds considered what to do, but there was only one way out—a traditional one from ancient times—namely to flee into the fertile Nile valley, which did not depend on rain, for there was enough water and grass there even in times of drought.
>
> And so these nomadic shepherds moved into neighboring Egypt. Once they arrived there, they settled—as usual for seminomads—at the border of the plain, not far from cultivated land. Here they came in contact with the Egyptians. The Egyptians tempted these nomadic shepherds and even succeeded in having them give up their nomadic lifestyle and work for them. At first these nomads rather liked the idea, since the Egyptians were experiencing prosperity at the time. Pharaoh Ramses II (1301–1234 B.C.E.) was in the process of building the cities of Ramses and Pithom. The Egyptians offered the nomadic shepherds the opportunity to work at the construction sites. The shepherds liked their new work at first; they started to earn a little. The Egyptians

were equally pleased to have finally found cheap foreign labor to help increase their own prosperity.

The semi-nomads began to experience bitter reality: working conditions were very hard; they were forced into serfdom; and they had no rights whatever. They were *habiru*, meaning "migrant groups of people with inferior rights who must serve others." In other words, these Habiru had no chance to speak out. They were simply to obey. After a while, the Egyptians even laid heavy taxes on them. They were forced to work longer for less pay. How else could the economic boom be achieved?

But all this was not enough for the Egyptians. They were increasingly frightened, feeling themselves threatened by the Habiru's lifestyle. They thought that if the Habiru continued to have so many children, they would become so numerous that they could in the future challenge the Egyptians' total rule and control over Egypt. Because of this fear of birthrate explosion, Pharaoh issued a decree ordering the killing of all male Hebrew children. The tragedy of the Hebrews reached its climax with this act.

As I was telling the story, one of my students spoke up: "But pastor, that's not the story of the Hebrews!"

"Whose story is it then?" I asked.

"That is the story of us Palestinians!" he answered. Before 1967, before Israel occupied the West Bank and Gaza, most Palestinians lived on the land. After 1967, Israel forced our people to stop farming and start working in construction. Thousands of Palestinians were hired as cheap construction workers by the Israelis. Despite their hard work, the Palestinian workers had no rights. After a while, especially after the 1980s, Palestinians were forced to pay high taxes to their occupiers. Israeli occupation grew more cruel every day. Thousands were arrested, hundreds were deported, and many children were murdered. All of this was done because of Israeli fear for their own security in the face of the birthrate explosion.

I was struck by my student's words. I was aware of the difference between our situation under Israeli occupation and the situation at the time of the Exodus. We are not "alien intruders" but a people who have lived in Palestine for thousands of years. It is much more a matter of vice-versa: It was the Israelis who came from outside and tried to drive us out by a variety of methods. Nor does our liberation consist in moving out of the land of oppression. On the contrary, we seek liberation from the oppressors in our land. Egypt, therefore, is not a geographical space to us but rather a description of our situation.

Despite these reservations, I was pleased with the words of my student. I became aware at that moment that the Exodus had become the present reality for this student. The history of its effects had reached my class. The biblical story was relevant to them; they had become participants in it.

Yet it is not enough to stop at this parallel between the circumstances of the Hebrews in Egypt and those of the Palestinians under Israeli occupation. We must continue reading the story. What is important in this story is God's attitude to that oppression. In the third chapter of Exodus we read, "And the Lord said, 'I have observed the misery of my people who are in Egypt; I have heard their cry on account of their taskmasters. Indeed, I know their sufferings'" (Exod 3:7).

The God of the Exodus is not a God who leaves the world to take care of itself. God remains true to the world. God follows what is happening in it. God is sensitive to what can be seen and heard. God is concerned. God knows what it means when a worker is exploited, when someone is deprived of his or her rights, or when children are denied life and future.

This God of the Exodus is the God we have come to know in Christ. A God who has himself suffered and therefore suffers with the suffering. A God who as a child had been oppressed by a Pharaoh named Herod and therefore is in solidarity with the refugee children. This is the God who was not afraid to cry out from the cross, "My God, my God, why have you forsaken me?" That is why he can understand the screams of the victims of violence. This is not a romantic God. God is not content to react emotionally—he acts. If he hears screams, he hurries to assist and to rescue (Exod 3:8).

This God also acts through human beings. That is why God calls people to follow and to participate actively in the process of liberation. God founded the first liberation movement on earth. In Exodus, God called Moses and ordered him to go to Pharaoh and tell him, "Let my people go. Let them move from serfdom into freedom."

Moses is a good example for the Christian community, which is called to be the voice of the voiceless, despite its own speech problems. It has the duty to seek out Pharaoh and talk to him. It has to convince him that oppression runs counter to God's will and will have bad consequences for him. If Pharaoh should ignore that word, then the church must dare to confront him.

The Bible is not a pious, esoteric book. It is quite realistic, as can be seen clearly in the Exodus story. In Exodus, we see Moses and Aaron standing before Pharaoh; we see the people as they start to move. At the same time, we see Pharaoh's attitude: obstinate, unmoved, inflexible. Indeed, he resorts to even stronger measures of oppression. He attempts to quell the insurrection by means of the iron fist. Those compromises that Pharaoh institutes from time to time are merely feints to gain time and to avoid the pressure of public opinion (Exod 8:8–10). He can only answer no to Moses' demand for freedom and independence. No to freedom, no to independence, and no to a state of their own.

How close is the parallel between Pharaoh's policy and Israel's! These no's of Pharaoh's are reminiscent of the three no's of Israel's former Prime Minister Shamir: "No to Palestinians' self determination! No to negotiations with the P.L.O.! And no to an independent state of Palestine!" How closely do Pharaoh's tactics in Exodus resemble those used by the Israeli occupation forces during the Intifada! Force, ever more force, but feints too. More and more Palestinians were becoming convinced that the end of Israeli occupation could not be achieved without economic sanctions by the United States and the European community. Nor did the Peace Conference have much chance of success without pressure from the United States. The Exodus would never have become reality without God's economic sanctions in Egypt (the ten plagues). Nor could apartheid in South Africa be ended without sanctions.

God's sanctions against Egypt finally led to the Hebrews' victory. The miracle occurred. The oppressed Hebrews succeeded in gaining their liberation despite Pharaoh's military superiority. Moses' sister Miriam commemorated it in song: "I will sing to the LORD, for he has triumphed gloriously; horse and rider he has thrown into the sea" (Exod 15:1). The freedom the Bible speaks of is not just "the freedom of the heart" but an all-encompassing freedom from all sins, be they sins of political oppression, sins of economic exploitation, or "sins of the heart." We apply the biblical concepts of freedom not only to free individuals but also to free societies.

But liberation in Holy Scripture refers not only to liberation from something but also liberation to something. That is why the Exodus story does not end with crossing through the Red Sea. On the contrary, the giving of the Ten Commandments follows right on its heels. The people liberated from Pharaoh received the Ten Commandments right after they were liberated, and the Ten Commandments refer to the Exodus first of all: "I am the LORD your God, who brought you out of the land of Egypt, out of the house of slavery" (Exod 20:2). The commandments exhort the liberated people to preserve the freedom they have already attained. It is not enough to gain freedom; one must be able to hold on to this freedom. Thus liberation brings with it ethical consequences, which is why the Old Testament people were repeatedly reminded not to forget the time of their enslavement in Egypt. "Remember that you too were a serf in the land of Egypt and that the LORD your God liberated you" is an exhortation often repeated in the Old Testament.

The need to recall the time of suffering in Egypt as the basis for life in the promised land could perhaps provide an essential starting point for a dialogue between Christian Palestinians and Jews. If the first task of the church is to order Pharaoh to grant freedom to oppressed people, then its second task is to help the liberated people preserve their freedom. The gospel of freedom also brings with it fruits of freedom. Liberation from oppression aims at a liberation to a life of righteousness. The teaching and preaching of the church awakens people to hear God's call to be free and to live accordingly. "For freedom Christ has set us free. Stand firm, therefore, and do not submit again to a yoke of slavery" (Gal 5:1). Paul's exhortation to the Galatians is also the exhortation of the Arab church in Palestine.

CHAPTER 10

# JONAH AND
# THE GULF CRISIS

IN PREACHING, it is important to pay attention to how a text is brought
into contact with the present. Our experiences of the world and of faith
direct us at particular times of our life to particular stories in Holy Scripture. We seek hope, assistance, comfort, or guidelines for coping with
one's own situation in these texts.

It is good to use Holy Scripture in this way, but it is also very dangerous. It is good, because this is how the Bible comes alive; dangerous,
because one could try to legitimize all kinds of ideologies on the basis of
the Bible. This means that in order to interpret Holy Scripture correctly
it is not only the manner of reading it but also the time it is being read
that is important. This fact was most evident to me during the Gulf crisis, as I shall try to explain.

It was the end of 1990, about five months after Iraq's invasion of
Kuwait. Several young people from our Bible study group came to me
and said they would like to read the book of Revelation with me. We had
had the habit every evening in our Bible study group of dealing with a
particular theme or scriptural passage about which the young people
wanted to learn more or which had bothered them.

The young people's wish to read the Revelation of John seemed
strange to me. I asked them what had brought this up and why they
were concerned with this particular book just now. One of the girls answered, "There are some people who derive the Gulf crisis from this
book. They say that there will soon be war in the Gulf, and that Iraq will
be destroyed as a result, and that it must happen because it is written in
Revelation. That's why we would like to read this passage together, to see
if this is true."

It was clear to me that my young people had met fundamentalists
who—as is typical—always look to Revelation at time of war in order
to appropriate history on that basis and so influence its course. As a

matter of fact, the number of fundamentalists grew like a cancerous tumor during the Gulf crisis. They applied several passages from Revelation directly to the Gulf crisis, using an interesting exegesis from the Apocalypse, appealing to chapters 16–19 in particular. Accordingly, Iraq was biblical Babylon. They found many of the war signs described in the seven bowls (Rev 16:1–21) such as, for example, the oil pollution in the Gulf in the second bowl (16:3), the waste gas and black clouds caused by the burning oil fields in the fifth bowl (16:10), and the deafening noise of the missile attacks in the lightning and thunder of the seventh bowl (16:18). Likewise, they were sure that the whole allied attack was conducted as the Bible had foreseen it and not only as the Americans had planned it. The terrible extent of the destruction also seemed to them to be "as it is written":

> Render to her as she herself has rendered,
>     and repay her double for her deeds;
>     mix a double draught for her in the cup she mixed (Rev 18:6).

The fundamentalists saw this war as a more or less just war willed by God. They were amazed at the accuracy of Scripture. It was this accuracy that confirmed them in their "right faith" and impelled them to become missionaries. They declared that this war was nothing less than the beginning of the end. It was the prelude to Christ's second coming. They drove people to repent, arguing that now their salvation was to be found only with the faithful band of fundamentalists.

This interpretation of Scripture is a tidy one and a dangerous one, for Scripture becomes a maker of war. The persecuted people's message of consolation becomes a frightening ideology. The testimony of faith turns into a dreadful enthusiasm. This interpretation isolates believers from the real world, inducing them to flee from history into their own inner world. It leads them to consider the cruelty of war inevitable.

The fundamentalists' interpretation of the Apocalypse showed me how necessary it is to read the Bible in its context. The book of Revelation is not the book of an attacking army but that of a persecuted Christian community. It became clear to me that when a biblical text is read it is important to take note of how it is read and by whom it is read.

I personally had had no interest in reading Revelation during the Gulf crisis. On the contrary, I had hit on another text in the Bible, one that seemed to me to be the proper message to be heard under the circumstances. It is the message of the prophet Jonah. I wanted to preach on this text the first Sunday after the outbreak of the war, but since all of Bethlehem had been placed under curfew at the time, I had to postpone it until three Sundays later.

Peter Arnett, the C.N.N. correspondent in Baghdad, showed some pictures of Iraq on television on that same Sunday. Among other things, he showed a church in Nineveh. A bomb had damaged the roof, dropped into the nave, and destroyed some church furniture and books. What remained was open to view. Some nuns and Iraqi Christians stood in the background; the priest was celebrating Mass at the altar. I found it interesting that the book of the prophet Jonah was being read in that church in Nineveh on that same Sunday. That confirmed my feeling that this book of the prophet was an important one to read in those days—by those Iraqi Christians as well as Palestinian Christians. But what, then, was its message? "Now the word of the LORD came to Jonah son of Amittai, saying, 'Go at once to Nineveh, that great city, and cry out against it; for their wickedness has come up before me' " (Jonah 1:1–2).

Jonah received the command from God to go to Nineveh—in today's Iraq—the capital of Assyria, and to "cry out against them." The prophet Jonah, an Israelite, was supposed to go to the capital of the empire which had long been one of Israel's greatest enemies, and which had even occupied the Northern Kingdom in the eighth century and deported its upper class.

But Jonah did not go. He fled instead, embarking on a ship leaving from Joppa, and headed toward Tarshish in Spain (1:3). The "convinced Zionist" Jonah, who believed in Israel's election, objected to presenting the Word to Nineveh the enemy. Jonah refused to go to Nineveh because he knew that if Nineveh should hear the word, believe it, and act accordingly, then God would show compassion. In plain words: if Nineveh believed the prophet's message it would be spared. Jonah could not stomach that thought, and so he fled.

But his attempt to escape failed. A storm overpowered the ship and calmed down only after the crew had cast Jonah overboard—at his own request. Jonah preferred to die rather than witness the enemy city remain undamaged. But a large fish swallowed Jonah and cast him ashore in three days. He could no longer avoid obeying God's command. So he went to Nineveh and preached the warning God had given him: "Forty days more, and Nineveh shall be overthrown!" Jonah preached against his will, one of the few preachers who hoped his sermon would find no hearers.

In order to see the reaction of the Nineveh inhabitants, Jonah settled down outside of town. But events took an unexpected turn: the king of Nineveh, the people, even the animals heeded the prophet's warning and repented. "When God saw what they did, how they turned from their evil ways, God changed his mind about the calamity that he had said he would bring upon them; and he did not do it" (3:10). What Jonah had feared really happened:

> But this was very displeasing to Jonah, and he became angry. He prayed to the LORD and said, "O LORD! Is not this what I said while I was still in my own country? That is why I fled to Tarshish at the beginning; for I knew that you are a gracious God and merciful, slow to anger, and abounding in steadfast love, and ready to relent from punishing. And now, O LORD, please take my life from me, for it is better for me to die than to live" (Jonah 4:1–3).

God did not want to leave Jonah like that, obdurate and sulky. He wanted Jonah to repent like Nineveh had. God, as a good father and imaginative teacher, wanted to make the divine decision comprehensible to Jonah:

> The LORD God appointed a bush, and made it come up over Jonah, to give him shade over his head, to save him from his discomfort; so Jonah was very happy about the bush. But when dawn came up the next day, God appointed a worm that attacked the bush, so that it withered. When the sun rose, God prepared a sultry east wind, and the sun beat down on the head of Jonah so that he was faint and asked that he might die. He said, "It is better for me to die than to live" (Jonah 4:6–8).

When God took pity on Jonah and appointed a bush, he made clear his pity on Nineveh:

> The LORD said, "You are concerned about the bush, for which you did not labor and which you did not grow; it came into being in a night and perished in a night. And should I not be concerned about Nineveh, that great city, in which there are more than a hundred

and twenty thousand persons who do not know their right hand
from their left, and also many animals?" (Jonah 4:10–11)

So God is not indifferent to Nineveh either—Israel's archenemy—but
on the contrary thinks it important. God grants it life rather than death
and destruction. God's compassion extends beyond Israel's borders. It encompasses the inhabitants of Nineveh and even its animals.

I was often reminded of the story of Jonah and Nineveh during the
Gulf crisis. I thought the attitude of the state of Israel (and of the United
States and the allies) toward Iraq was like Jonah's attitude toward Nineveh. The United States and Israel (even if Israel did not participate directly in the last war) wished to avoid any serious conversation with Iraq,
if at all possible. They made every effort to avoid negotiating with the
Iraqi government to convince them to leave Kuwait. The sanctions ordered by the United Nations were allotted neither sufficient time nor sufficient space to be effective. In my opinion, the war could have been
avoided—even on February 23, 1991, when the allies began their ground
attack on the same day that Iraq agreed to the Soviet plan. Israel, which
had feared until then that the crisis might perhaps end peacefully, cheered
at the start of the ground attack.

On that day, February 23, 1991, it became obvious to the world
that the real goal of the war was not what had first been stated, namely,
the liberation of Kuwait. The actual goal was the destruction of Iraq as
an economic and military power in the region. Saddam Hussein had
done wrong in occupying Kuwait, but the allied plan was to ruin him
totally and destroy his land as well as his army, rather than just to drive
him out of Kuwait. The infrastructure of Iraq was destroyed in order to
put an end to the occupation of Kuwait. It was the civilian population,
not Saddam Hussein, who had to bear the consequences of the war.

So Iraq was to be destroyed, for only one nation has the right to be
powerful in the Middle East; only one nation is allowed to be equipped
with weapons of destruction; only one nation is permitted to occupy
territory—Israel. Could this be a new version of the election of Israel?

Just as Jonah denied Nineveh the right to live, so did Israel, the
United States, and the allies deny Iraq the right to live. Even the Israeli
peace movement, which had raised a prophetic voice during the Intifada,
was in favor of the war in the Gulf. Pity on Iraq was not evident. Pity
on sea birds, yes. The picture of the sea bird that could no longer move
because it was covered with oil touched the world's sentiments, just as

Jonah had pity on the bush. But who had pity on the Iraqi people who had been subjected to 100,000 bombing raids? Who had pity on those who were suddenly deprived of electricity, water, and functioning drains, and had to spend the cold days and nights of January and February deprived of these basic necessities—and who will probably have to do without for quite a while longer? Who had pity on the Iraqi mothers who lost their sons at the front or in bunkers? In any case, there were very few reports of casualties. Only the numbers were announced—not always—but not their faces or those of their grieving relatives. The war seemed like a thrilling computer game on television. All human features were blurred, for discomfort to the viewer must be avoided at all costs. The world's public must not be turned against the war through pity.

Who cares about Iraq? Everyone was drunk with victory. That was glory for the West. Only the God who loves humanity cares about Iraq. God is not indifferent to the Iraqi population. God has compassion for that great nation in which eighteen million persons live "who do not know their right hand from their left" (Jonah 4:11).

The interesting fact about the book of Jonah is that it was written several centuries after the destruction of Nineveh. Nineveh was destroyed in the year 612 B.C.E., but the book of Jonah was probably written in the fourth century B.C.E. It is as though it had been written for today's Jews, so that they could learn from their history and their prophet.

But it was also written for the Christians; it is contained in their Bible. I am afraid that neither the Jews nor the Western Christians learned a thing from the message of this prophet. Nineveh was destroyed once again.

How many Ninevehs must yet be destroyed before we human beings learn? Are we capable of learning at all? When will we grasp the fact that God's compassion really has no limits, that it encompasses everyone, and that no one is excluded from it?

# CHAPTER 11
# LOVE YOUR ENEMY

## The Good Samaritan

ONE OF THE most beautiful parables in the Bible is the one concerning the Good Samaritan in Luke 10:25–37.

> Just then a lawyer stood up to test Jesus. "Teacher" he said, "what must I do to inherit eternal life?" He said to him, "What is written in the law? What do you read there?" He answered, "You shall love the Lord your God with all your heart, and with all your soul, and with all your strength, and with all your mind; and your neighbor as yourself." And he said to him, "You have given the right answer; do this, and you will live."
>
> But wanting to justify himself, he asked Jesus, "And who is my neighbor?" Jesus replied, "A man was going down from Jerusalem to Jericho, and fell into the hands of robbers, who stripped him, beat him, and went away, leaving him half dead. Now by chance a priest was going down that road; and when he saw him, he passed by on the other side. So likewise a Levite, when he came to the place and saw him, passed by on the other side. But a Samaritan while traveling came near him; and when he saw him, he was moved with pity. He went to him and bandaged his wounds, having poured oil and wine on them. Then he put him on his own animal, brought him to an inn, and took care of him. The next day he took out two denarii, gave them to the innkeeper, and said, 'Take care of him; and when I come back, I will repay you whatever more you spend.' Which of these three, do you think, was a neighbor to the man who fell into the hands of the robbers?" He said, "The one who showed him mercy." Jesus said to him, "Go and do likewise."

This parable was interpreted differently at different times. One of the oldest interpretations was an allegorical one; it originated here in the Near East and was popular until the early Middle Ages. A deep salvation-historical meaning was attributed to the words. According to this interpretation, the man behind the man leaving Jerusalem in Luke 10:30 was none other than Adam, meaning every single human being. Jerusalem was the symbol for paradise. Jericho, which is located on low ground, was the world. The robber attack was simply:

> the work of the hostile and dark demonic and satanic powers who rob the person of spiritual gifts of grace, of eternal life, innocence, and likeness to God as though these things were clothes, beat him with moral shortcomings and sins, and leave him half dead and half alive—thus in large measure incapable of saving himself—to his fate. Nor can priests and Levites (Luke 10:31–32) help. They and their weakness embody law and prophets, priesthood and temple cult, functionaries of Old Testament legalism, possibly even the periods before and after the Mosaic Law was handed down.
>
> Only the Samaritan of Luke 10:33 can accomplish the rescue, for hiding behind him is Christ the guardian, shepherd, and physician. With oil and wine, mild and strong medicines, with sacred ointment, baptism and Eucharist, with consolation and exhortation, with forgiving grace and heavy penance, the heavenly rescuer in Luke 10:34–35 begins the process of healing and restoration. When the Samaritan loads the wounded man on his own animal to bring him to the nearest inn, this means metaphorically that Christ has become man for his sake and that . . . God has assumed the suffering on the cross that reconciles humankind. What follows leads back to the Christian community, which admits all persons of goodwill and provides them with the correct faith through its leaders—be they apostles, presbyters, bishops, prelates, pastors, teachers, or deacons. The Samaritan's promise to return and pay any added expenses is interpreted in the sense of the parousia and the last judgment, whereby the added work done by those responsible for the community is seen above all in the development of new teachings, exhortations and advice not contained in the Bible but contained in the exegetical and homiletical praxis as well as in the fulfillment of various special requests.[1]

This interpretation is still in use in Palestine, not only in the Greek Orthodox and Catholic churches but also in several Protestant churches. As a result, it was very familiar to me in my childhood. However, other interpretations were being disseminated in Palestine, which understand the text literally rather than allegorically. And I was also confronted with this parable during my studies in Germany and there learned to read it in the historical-critical sense.

In spite of all these different interpretations, this text was never so close to me as during the Intifada. One particular incident that took place around Bethlehem reminded me very forcibly of this parable. Because of this story I could begin to sense what such a parable could have meant in Luke's time.

The event took place on April 5, 1990. That evening a cold wind was blowing over Jerusalem and Bethlehem. Ariel and Hariel, two Jewish children, were standing at a bus stop on one of the Jerusalem streets. The ten-year-old children were on their way home. A bus stopped, and the two children, busy talking, got on. They did not notice they had gotten on the wrong bus until the last stop, when they noticed they had landed in a totally different place. The frightened children asked the Jewish bus driver for help, but he had no time for them. It was quitting time. So as to lose no more time, he ordered the children to get off and ask someone on the street for help. The children had no choice but to say good night and descend from the bus, leaving them stranded on a deserted street far south in Jerusalem in the dark. They saw a well-lit thoroughfare not far from the bus stop and ran to it, deciding to walk along on it in the hope of finding someone who would help.

This road was the Hebron road, which starts at the Jaffa Gate and leads to Hebron by way of Bethlehem. The children walked—toward the south instead of north. With every step they took it got darker, quieter, and colder. The children became more and more uneasy and nervous. After about four hours of walking, it became obvious to them that they were going the wrong way. They had already covered ten kilometers without getting any nearer their goal.

At about 9:30 that evening the children passed a gas station, where a light was still burning. A twenty-five-year-old man was standing outside the station. "Finally a human being, finally a rescuer," the children thought. The station looked a bit Arabic, as did the surroundings. The two Jewish children became scared; they were wearing caps (*kipas*), a sign that they belonged to a pious Jewish family. But when they noticed that they were in an Arab neighborhood, they took their caps off and hid them. Cautiously they approached the young Arab and addressed him in Hebrew. He answered in Hebrew. They asked him if they could call their parents, and he led them into the station. He placed the telephone in the office at their disposal. One of the children dialed his parents' number, and the mother answered.

"Where are you, Ariel?" she asked, by now desperate, furious, and very worried.

"We got lost," answered Ariel.

"Where are you now?"

"I don't know for sure, but I'll let you talk to the young man from the gas station. He can tell you where we are."

"Hello, here is Isa. Your children arrived here a few minutes ago totally beat. They got lost. But you need not worry anymore. I'll take good care of them."

The Jewish mother noticed, from the young man's accent, that she was talking with an Arab. She asked him where he was and how one could find the service station.

"Very simple," Isa told her. "Do you know the Dehesha refugee camp? The gas station is exactly on the opposite side of the road."

The mother couldn't believe her ears. Had her children really fallen into the hands of Palestinians in Dehesha? She knew exactly what Dehesha was like. Dehesha is one of the largest Palestinian camps in the West Bank, and the resistance of its inhabitants to Israeli occupation is very strong. She knew that the Palestinians living there had been driven out of their villages in 1948 at the time Israel was founded, and that they had been forced to live in this refugee camp ever since. This Jewish mother knew well how badly off these Palestinians were and that they were being treated like animals by the Israeli soldiers. Because she knew all this, she was very frightened. Would her children be treated humanely by this oppressed Palestinian? Would they get out of that gas station alive? Moreover, what this mother did not know was who Isa really was. She did not know that he had lost six members of his family to Israeli violence. The last of the six had been his cousin Ali, who had died in the Israeli prison Nafha after a long hunger strike.

The Jewish mother feared for her children. She called several men she knew and begged them to drive to Dehesha to pick up the two children. But she herself stayed by the telephone. Every five minutes she called the gas station to ask how the children were and to beg Isa not to hurt them.

The two children were Isa's chance to revenge himself on the Israelis. This would be a unique opportunity to punish the Israelis for years of oppression and make them suffer for the life of suffering he was forced to lead. But Isa did not do it. He took pity on them; he made the telephone available to them. He noticed that they were freezing and turned on the electric heater for them. He knew they had not eaten in a long time and so he ran home and brought them something to eat and drink. He took pains to make them feel at home.

The story reminded me strongly of the story of the Good Samaritan. The Jewish children in trouble found no help from their compatriot the bus driver. Of all people, it was a Palestinian, a man belonging to the enemy camp, one who was despised and oppressed by the Israelis—of all people it was he who helped these two Israeli children who were in trouble. Of all of them, it was a Muslim, a man who is not a member of the Jewish religion—of all people it was he who helped the two pious Jewish children. The Palestinian realized that in this situation the children were no longer enemies; they were neighbors who need help. The Palestinian became a neighbor to the two Jewish children on that day.

The story did not make the headlines, of course. It was not shown on television, for no blood had been shed. The story was therefore "unprofitable." Only two newspapers, one Israeli and one Palestinian, reported it.

This story is gospel, a message of love for one's enemy. Of all people, it was a Palestinian Muslim who recognized the will of God. Of all people, it was he who saw a neighbor when he looked at his "enemy" in trouble, one who merited and needed his love. In this case, loving one's enemy was not an ideal that the young Palestinian was trying to achieve. It was a concrete deed in a concrete situation.

## Loving One's Enemy and Resistance

Christian Palestinians are often placed in a very difficult quandary: the European and American Christians accuse them of nationalism and the extremist Arabs accuse them of lack of patriotism. If the former demand that they love their enemy, the latter demand militant resistance on their part. What can they do?

The commandment to love one's enemy is an essential part of the

Christian faith. The Christian is dutybound to follow the Lord as model and thus to love the enemy. This kind of love is not some sentimental response, nor is it an abstract concept. To love one's enemy does not mean one accepts everything the enemy dishes out. It does not mean watching passively while injustice is being perpetrated. It certainly does not mean becoming resigned to the behavior of the enemy or, worse still, collaborating with the enemy. To love one's enemy means neither to cover up the conflict nor to downplay its seriousness, but rather to endure the tension inherent in that conflict without succumbing to hatred. One should love the persons but not the unjust acts they commit. To love one's enemy means, therefore, that despite the conflict one recognizes the enemy as a creature of God who has a right to live, to be forgiven, and to love—but not the right to commit an unjust act.

As Palestinians, we have nothing against Jews for being Jews. But we do have something against them insofar as they are an alien occupation force in the West Bank and Gaza who suppress us and occupy our land against our will. If we keep silent about the behavior of the Israeli army in the occupied territories, it does not mean we love our enemy; it is rather a rift in brotherly love. And if we then raise our voices against the injustice that the state of Israel inflicts on us Palestinians, it is not because we are anti-Semitic—since we ourselves are Semites too—but because we see it as imperiling our faith in God the Creator of all human beings. Anti-Semitism, like all other racist ideologies, wounds God the Creator, for all human beings without exception are created in the image of God. God encounters us in every human being, whether American, European, Israeli, or Palestinian.

God forbids us to shed our enemy's blood. But God also summons us to resist our enemy, if that enemy attempts to shed the blood of our neighbor. We do not want to kill our enemy, but we will not let him kill our brother or sister either. Loving one's enemy without resisting him would be a cheap, abstract, and treasonable attitude. But to resist without loving one's enemy can be inhuman, brutal, and violent. The one without the other would violate divine and human rights. But if we can endure the tension, both love and resistance offer the only way out for us Christians.

The Palestinian Intifada has achieved very much in this respect. It has eliminated two fears at the same time: fear of resisting and fear of talking to the enemy. Never in their history had the Palestinian people been more ready to resist as in the Intifada. At the same time, never have so many Palestinians talked with Jews and Israelis as during the Intifada. The Palestinians have thus shown that they can still forgive the enemy and regard the enemy as a creature of God, despite the injustice done to them.

Yet this must not happen at the cost of the Palestinians' own right to a life lived in peace, to independence, and to justice. We do not demand vengeance; we demand justice. We are required to love our enemy but not at the cost of our brother or sister. Loving our enemy drives us to resist injustice. But resistance requires that we love our enemy if we are not to sink into racism and ideology. Criticism of Israel must always include self-criticism. That can occur only when faith hones one's conscience and love guides one's reason.

# CHAPTER 12

# CHRISTIAN REALITY IN PALESTINE

## Christmas in Bethlehem

CHRISTMAS EVE in Bethlehem—that was always something special. The city always started to prepare for this feast one month beforehand. The streets were decorated with colored lights and colorful figures. Christmas trees could be seen everywhere in the stores. St. Nicholas sought out the children to bestow gifts on them.

The climax always occurred on the morning of the respective Christmas Eve (in Bethlehem, Christmas was celebrated three times: the Latin church celebrated on December 25; the Orthodox on January 6; and the Armenians on January 18) when the Patriarch arrived. All the celebrities of the city and surroundings would then set out to receive the Patriarch and his retinue at the entrance to the city. Accompanied by riders, scouts, and large crowds, the Patriarch's entourage would slowly make its way through the narrow streets, with the whole population waving greetings from the sidelines.

Upon reaching the site of the crib, the Patriarch would be greeted by the mayor of Bethlehem and the representatives of the various churches, while the bells of the Church of the Nativity peeled their greeting.

This was the custom in Bethlehem. This is how Christmas was usually celebrated. But circumstances had changed by December 1987. The Intifada had just begun. The Palestinians were groaning under the yoke of Israeli occupation. Many Palestinians had been shot dead by Israeli soldiers. Sadness overshadowed Bethlehem as never before. So Christmas Eve 1987 in Bethlehem was, contrary to custom, very quiet:

> The roads [to Bethlehem] mourn
> for no one comes to the festivals;
> all her gates are desolate,

> her priests groan, her young girls grieve
> and her lot is bitter (Lam 1:4).

All Christmas celebrations were canceled. No appearance of the Patriarch, and no reception of him, no St. Nicholas, no decorated Christmas tree, no shining lights, and no Palestinian Christians on the streets. Only a few foreigners could be seen here and there. As for the rest, the city teemed with Israeli soldiers.

The following sentence was spray-painted on the wall of our Lutheran school two days before Christmas: "Excuse us, dear Christ, unfortunately we cannot celebrate your birthday this year, for we are an occupied people whose children are denied life!"

I used that sentence in my Christmas sermon. I told the congregation that we really felt we could not celebrate the birthday of a child prodigy descended from heaven. That would indeed be a bit much. Nor did we feel like greeting Santa Claus and opening gifts.

> But we could really do without that for a while; there is no mention of any of it in the Bible. Instead, Holy Scripture relates the story of a refugee child who has nowhere to lay his head. It is a truly human child, one who is not born into a beautiful, rosy, peaceful world but into a cruel world just like ours. The biblical Christmas story tells of the birth of a child who was denied life too and who was forced to fear for his life. A child born at the time of Herod the Great, who had ordered the slaying of all the children in the vicinity of Bethlehem. A child who became a refugee very early in his life.
>
> Yet God comes into the world in, through, and with this child. God himself becomes like our Palestinian refugees. He becomes one of us, one who was driven from his homeland. God is very close to us precisely at this time of occupation. Furthermore, he understands our suffering like no other because he himself underwent these sufferings. He felt them in his own body. So we have not been deserted even in this terrible situation. There is one who went down this road before us so that we should not have to go alone. God enters this world as a very small and powerless baby; but just so he overcomes this world.
>
> That is why we Christian Palestinians must, especially now, commemorate Christmas. Christmas is nothing but the prologue of the crucified one. And we who bear our cross believe in the crucified

one, for we know from him that he accompanies us on our way and does not desert us. Because God appeared in the depth of night, our night cannot be sad. That is why we can and indeed must celebrate Christmas, albeit not as usual. Not with splendor but with the refugee child of Bethlehem whose story is told in Holy Scripture. Only then will we celebrate Christmas correctly. Perhaps it is precisely now, under the occupation, that we can best understand the mystery of the child driven out of Bethlehem.

Thus Christmas 1987 was transformed into a true and meaningful Christ-Mass.

## Giving the Enemy One's Cloak as Well

No text in either the New or the Old Testament has so fascinated and so disturbed the church as the Sermon on the Mount. Throughout the history of the church, the question has repeatedly surfaced as to how to interpret the words of Jesus in Matthew 5–7. One wonders whether these exhortations could really be obeyed. They seem to be too radical, too utopian, and much too unrealistic.

In the course of the centuries several attempts were made to dissolve this radicality. Many theologians of the ancient and medieval church, for example, attempted to distinguish between what Jesus demanded from the perfect Christians and what he demanded from ordinary Christians. The perfect Christians obey all the commandments of the Sermon on the Mount, but the ordinary Christians can do only as much as they are able.

Martin Luther, on the other, hand, emphasized that the Sermon on the Mount must be seen in the light of law and gospel, or rather of the doctrine of the two kingdoms. On the one hand, the words show us that we cannot obey them with our own strength. On the other hand, they show us the fruits produced by the person justified by faith. That is why Luther made the distinction between person-in-Christ and person-in-the-world the key to interpreting the Sermon on the Mount.

As long as it concerns only himself, the Christian is totally bound by the demand of the Sermon on the Mount to offer the other cheek and not resist evil; but insofar as he occupies a secular office such as prince or head of family, he is required to protect his land or his family and thus resist evil.

The social and political relevance of the Sermon on the Mount was increasingly stressed in this century, and even more so after World War II. Issues of the right to resist, pacifism, and refusal to serve in the military were associated with the Sermon on the Mount. Socio-political figures like Mohandas Gandhi and Martin Luther King, Jr., appealed in part to the Sermon on the Mount in their nonviolent struggles for the rights of Indians and blacks.

I have no wish to present a new interpretation of the Sermon on the Mount. Rather, I will relate a story that could pertain to Matthew 5:40, the passage containing one of Jesus' most difficult demands: "And if anyone wants to sue you and take your coat, give your cloak as well."

We Christian Palestinians find these demands of Jesus troublesome. We wonder about their real meaning. Is this demand valid, comprehensible, and capable of being carried out by believing individuals only, or can it be applied to a group of people as well? A few naive Christians have sometimes asked us to obey this demand and relinquish the West Bank and the Gaza Strip, thus resolving our quarrel with Israel. Seen in that way, the Sermon on the Mount seems like a gigantic summons to surrender, to renounce every human right—indeed, to condone evil.

Yet the following story poses the possibility that these words of Jesus are also an exhortation to resist—a resistance that must be carried out by nonviolent means, of course. I know that this is not a new idea, but I would like to present it in light of an example from recent Palestinian history.

It was the fall of 1989. The Intifada had just achieved one of its successes. The more or less nonviolent resistance of the Palestinians was growing. It was at this time that the Palestinian village of Beit Sahour, two kilometers from Bethlehem, made the headlines.

The name "Beit Sahour" has for centuries been connected with the place where the shepherds were told the good news of the Messiah's birth in Bethlehem. Today, Beit Sahour is now a small city with about 10,000 inhabitants. More than 80 percent of them are Christians, the other 20 percent are Muslims. The majority of the Christians are Greek Orthodox; small Catholic and Lutheran congregations were also established in the last one hundred years.

Beit Sahour, still a small, very poor, tumbledown place of 600 inhabitants during the last century, transformed itself into one of the most thriving cities in Palestine. Two factors influenced this development: industry and education.

The city contains many large factories. The plastics factory of Beit Sahour, for instance, is one of the largest in all the Arab world. The noodle factory is the biggest in Palestine. There are several large, and many small textile, wood, and mother-of-pearl works here.

As for education—the Lutheran schools play a large role in this achievement—Beit Sahour is noted for having one of the highest per capita concentrations of Palestinians with college degrees.

This small and lively city was encircled by Israeli armed forces in the autumn of 1989. All streets leading into or out of the city were blocked with large rocks and dry fill. A strict curfew was imposed on the whole city. For almost forty days no inhabitant was permitted to leave the city. Nor were inhabitants allowed to leave their own houses. Beit Sahour and its inhabitants were completely cut off from the rest of the world. All telephone lines in the city were cut. Neither European consuls, nor Arab members of the Knesset, nor Christian heads of churches in Jerusalem were allowed to visit the city. The Israeli military forces had declared the city a military restricted zone. Former Israeli Minister of Defense Yitzhak Rabin announced that he intended "to teach" the inhabitants of Beit Sahour "a lesson." Why these punitive measures? Why did Beit Sahour have to be punished?

Beit Sahour wanted to participate in the Palestinian insurrection by boycotting their tax payments to the military government. The executive committee of the Intifada had recommended the tax boycott as early as 1987, but nowhere else was it carried out as efficiently as in Beit Sahour. All the inhabitants participated as one unit.

The citizens of Beit Sahour justified their tax boycott with two slogans, "No taxation under occupation" and "No taxation without representation." These slogans were presented with greater detail in a circulated handbill:

> We consider the occupation of one people by another people a clear violation of international laws and religions. It is contrary to simple human rights and to democracy. The Israeli policy of collecting taxes contradicts international agreements, the Geneva and the Hague conventions in particular. In the twenty-two years of occupation, the Israeli authorities have not yet rendered an accounting of tax distributions in the West Bank.
>
> Since the beginning of the occupation of the West Bank and Gaza Strip, the authorities have instituted new kinds of taxes that

have never existed before, like the luxury tax, VAT, taxes on stones, and this in itself contradicts all Geneva and the Hague conventions.

We firmly believe that every citizen should pay taxes to his national government so that it can carry out its duties and obligations; we therefore ask, 'Where is our national government?' Where are the social services? They are almost nonexistent. There is no social insurance, no old-age home, no home for the handicapped, no orphanage.

Regarding medical care: health care in the West Bank still harks back to the nineteenth century, especially our hospitals and medicines. And they are not free. The authorities have established a voluntary but expensive health insurance. The people who can afford to pay for this insurance constitute less than 10 percent of the population. Statistics have shown that the money paid into this health insurance is three times as much as the medical care costs in the West Bank.

Regarding education: there are no free schools for our children in the West Bank, despite our school taxes. Our school children pay fees and buy their own books. Furthermore, there are no state universities in the West Bank and Gaza Strip, and existing universities have been closed for more than two years.

As far as our natural resources are concerned, control over our water sources has been taken over by force by Israel. They have decreased the amount of water delivered, and sold us the surplus for very high prices. They have diverted water to their settlements in the West Bank.

The city administrations in our cities suffer from enormous deficits, which mirror the occupation authorities' neglect of services rendered.

For these reasons—and as a consequence of our conviction that the money taken in by the high taxes we pay is spent on ammunition and tear gas used to kill our children—we have decided not to pay taxes anymore.[1]

The inhabitants of Beit Sahour were therefore punished for this nonviolent resistance. This Christian city was to be taught a lesson precisely because of this "civil disobedience." That is why the city was cut off and its inhabitants rendered prisoners in their own houses.

During the fall of 1989, the Israeli military started to cart away trucks loaded with household goods, video sets, TV sets, washing machines, refrigerators, and other things from private households and from shops. During those days goods valued at more than $1,800,000 were confiscated from these recalcitrant inhabitants of Beit Sahour. Moreover, tax boycotters who protested were arrested and forced to spend considerable time in prison.

One day during this time, the tax collectors, supported by the Israeli military, pushed their way into one of the houses in Beit Sahour. They started to move everything out, loading the family's possessions onto a large truck. The family stood and watched as their furniture, acquired so painstakingly piece by piece whenever they could afford it, was being hauled away. Each piece of furniture called up stories, reminiscences, and the memory of the sweat it had cost them. After a few hours, the living room was totally empty. The soldiers, after having robbed her of all her possessions, turned to bid farewell to the elderly owner, a Christian. The old woman looked at the young soldier sadly. Her glance contained suffering, pain, and rage. Her lips moved, but not to curse, not to cry out, not even to scold.

"You forgot the curtains. Please do not forget to take them down too and remove them."

An eerie silence descended on the room. Shamed and guilty, the soldiers left. They took everything except the curtains. At that moment the old woman had achieved dignity. At that moment the triumphant Israeli army had lost the battle. An old woman had defeated them. She gave her enemy, who wanted to sue her and take her dress, her coat also. That became reality. That was resistance.

# CONCLUSION:
# I HAVE A DREAM

IN 1988, ENCOURAGED by the Palestinian National Council's Declaration of Independence of the State of Palestine, I dared to dream a dream. This dream of a "two-states solution" is not an ideological concept, not a rigid structure, and not definitive. It is well known that dreams have no boundaries. Nor should this dream have a rigid boundary; it is a dream that can still be dreamed, but it also cries out for a greater dream. The most important question is still: Does this dream have the strength to set something in motion? Will it remain a pious wish or will it make history?

Some years have passed since I dreamed the dream. I hope it is not outdated already; it was already a daring risk at the time because, as I said then, "The attempt is to take two steps into the daylight of the future even though we are still standing in the darkness of the present."

I am a Palestinian living under Israeli occupation. My captor daily seeks ways to make life harder for me. He encircles my people with barbed wire; he builds walls around us, and his army sets many boundaries around us. He succeeds in keeping thousands of us in camps and prisons.

Yet despite all these efforts, he has not succeeded in taking my dreams from me. He could not imprison them. His suppression could not keep me from thinking of a joint future with him. His brutality against the Intifada did not succeed in discouraging me from dreaming of a peaceful coexistence with him. I have a dream that I cherish and care for like my own child. But this dream is being born into a world full of nightmares.

I have a dream that I will one day wake up and see two equal peoples living next to each other, coexisting in the land of Palestine, stretching from the Mediterranean to the Jordan. These two peoples have learned to share this small strip of land. They have allowed themselves to be convinced that their destinies can no longer be kept separate and that the only possibilities they have are common survival or mutual destruction.

The Israel of which I dream is an Israel no longer seduced by the voices of false prophets, meaning that it no longer clings to dreams of a Greater Israel and no longer acts like an expansionist colonial power in the Middle East. On the contrary, it is an Israel that has learned to accommodate itself to the structure of the Middle East and to adapt to its environment without, however, losing its identity as a nation, a people, and a religion.

The Palestine I see before me is a Palestine that does not allow any Arab or Western state to determine its future. A Palestine that has learned that history cannot be reversed, and that Israel is a part of both present and future history. This dream began to assume reality in the Intifada after the Palestinians took their destiny into their own hands and proposed a two-states solution.

I have a dream of two peoples who are not separated by a wall. The Berlin wall is already past history. The time of the Cold War is over—I hope not only in Europe and the northern hemisphere. A truce and small wars no longer satisfy us. What both peoples need is peace: a real, just, and true peace.

Israel needs this peace to avoid becoming a nuclear ghetto, living in splendid isolation in the Middle East. Palestine needs the peace in order to be able to live next to mighty Israel without fear. The security of both peoples can only be guaranteed by a just peace. Without peace there is no security and no survival.

The Jerusalem of which I dream no longer has an Almond Tree Gate to separate the east and the west sides. It is an open city, large enough to take both peoples under its wing. Its small streets and thoroughfares are broad enough to carry adherents of all three monotheistic religions and persons of all nations. It will be a city about which the Psalmist said, "the tribes go up to it" (Ps 122:3):

> For I am about to create Jerusalem as a joy,
>     and its people as a delight. . . .
> no more shall the sound of weeping be heard in it,
>     or the cry of distress. . . .
> They shall build houses and inhabit them;

they shall plant vineyards and eat their fruit.
They shall not build and another inhabit;
    they shall not plant and another eat. . . .
They shall not labor in vain
    or bear children for calamity. . . .
They shall not hurt or destroy
    on all my holy mountain
    says the LORD (Isa 65:18–25).

I have a dream of two peoples who live side by side in peace with one another and so do not need to waste their vast resources on weapons which will just rust away. These two peoples would not expend their energy on the arms race, but would instead compete in building a healthy economy grounded in social justice.

The sufferings and persecutions undergone by both peoples have also created many social needs and problems among them, the solution to which will cost both states dearly in terms of money and energy. But these sufferings and persecutions have also refined both peoples. Both have delved deeply into science from the best sources in the world; both have fine talents and possibilities at their disposal. What a blessing this would be for the Middle East if both peoples would combine their scientific efforts! What an economic powerhouse could be built here! What a seductive oasis could be created here, attracting all nations! And, piece by piece, what Micah wrote would be fulfilled:

In days to come
    the mountain of the LORD's house
shall be established as the highest of the mountains,
    and shall be raised up above the hills.
Peoples shall stream to it,
    and many nations shall come and say:
"Come, let us go up to the mountain of the LORD,
    to the house of the God of Jacob;
that he may teach us his ways
    and that we may walk in his paths."
For out of Zion shall go forth instruction,
    and the word of the LORD from Jerusalem.
He shall judge between many peoples,
    and shall arbitrate between strong nations far away;

they shall beat their swords into plowshares,
 and their spears into pruning hooks;
nation shall not lift up sword against nation,
 neither shall they learn war any more (Micah 4:1–3).

I have a dream about two peoples in whom one can see the cradle
of three monotheistic religions. It can be seen not only in the ancient stones
of the Wailing Wall, of the Church of the Resurrection, and of the Dome
of the Rock, but in the people themselves—Jews, Christians, and Muslims. A bit of the divinity of their God is evidenced in their dealings
with each other, in the way they use the freedom and power granted to
them.

I think of two peoples who keep the name of God holy and do not
misuse it to further their own interests or suppress others. The fact that
they obey God's law is made evident by how they obey and protect
human rights. I have a dream of two peoples who daily carry out what
is written in the Declarations of Independence of their respective states,
two peoples who respect, honor, and protect the freedom of religion and
opinion of all their citizens—Jews, Christians, Muslims, religious people as well as atheists, liberals as well as fundamentalists. The freedom
to express themselves and to progress is given to all, though the freedom
to interfere with the freedom of others is denied to all.

I have a dream of two peoples who work closely together to ame-
liorate and heal the wounds of their members and citizens. The trauma
of the Holocaust roused many fears in the Jews that need to be overcome.
The wounds of the Palestinian refugees and exiles are still bleeding and
cry out for healing. Both peoples need to be cured of fear, bitterness, mis-
trust, and pain. It will take the exertions of all of us to achieve the goal
of having everyone thinking in terms of a common future and working
for it—the young Palestinian demonstrators and the Israeli soldiers who
shoot them, the Palestinian prisoners and their Israeli prison guards, the
Palestinians and Israelis full of fear.

Yet that must not be the end of my dream. On the contrary, I dream
that—after a period of nationalism—we begin to think in international
terms and that a commonwealth of all states is created in the Near East,
with Israel, Palestine, Jordan, Lebanon, Syria, Iraq, Saudi Arabia, and the
Gulf states as members. Each of these can have its own state, in which
each people can exercise its sovereign rights. Yet all these states are nevertheless allied in a primarily economic bond. These states will shake the

dust of the East-West conflict from their feet, develop common interests, and set out to improve the region so that justice and prosperity will be available to all. These states will have learned that the future of one cannot be attained at the cost of the others, and that security for one can never be achieved at the cost of others. They are states that are grateful for their God-given riches and use them accordingly, for the welfare of all their citizens.

Now that the Cold War that had splintered the Middle East is ended, and a peace agreement, however fragile, has been forged, even if there are not many results as yet, my dream is no longer a total illusion. If these efforts break down or if one side manipulates all the others, then the North-South conflict will come through the Middle East, causing constant instability and letting no one have peace.

That is my dream. I ask, "Is it too beautiful to be real? Is it too reasonable to become reality?"

That is my dream. It is no longer an illusion if people find it believable. If people work to achieve it, the reality is no longer very far off. But if it is abandoned, then all of us—really all of us—will sink into a terrible nightmare.

# APPENDICES

## 1. Declaration of Independence of the State of Palestine

*In the name of God, the Compassionate, the Merciful*

DECLARATION OF INDEPENDENCE

Palestine, the land of the three monotheistic religions, is where the Palestinian Arab people was born, on which it grew, developed, and excelled. The Palestinian people was never separated from or diminished in its integral bonds with Palestine. Thus the Palestinian Arab people ensured for itself an everlasting union between itself, its land, and its history.

Resolute throughout that history, the Palestinian Arab people forged its national identity, rising even to unimagined levels in its defense, as invasion, the design of others, and the special appeal to Palestine's ancient and luminous place on that eminence where powers and civilizations are joined. . . . All this intervened thereby to deprive the people of its political independence. Yet the undying connection between Palestine and its people secured for the land its character, and for the people its national genius.

Nourished by an unfolding series of civilizations and cultures, inspired by a heritage rich in variety and kind, the Palestinian Arab people added to its stature by consolidating a union between itself and its patrimonial land. The call went out from temple, church, and mosque that to praise the Creator, to celebrate compassion and peace was indeed the message of Palestine. And in generation after generation, the Palestinian Arab people gave of itself unsparingly in the valiant battle for liberation and homeland. For what has been the unbroken chain of our people's rebellions but the heroic embodiment of our will for national independence? And so the people was sustained in the struggle to stay and to prevail.

117

When in the course of modern times a new order of values was declared with norms and values fair for all, it was the Palestinian Arab people that had been excluded from the destiny of all other peoples by a hostile array of local and foreign powers. Yet again had unaided justice been revealed as insufficient to drive the world's history along its preferred course.

And it was the Palestinian people, already wounded in its body that was submitted to yet another type of occupation over which floated the falsehood that "Palestine was a land without people." This notion was foisted upon some in the world, whereas in Article 22 of the Covenant of the League of Nations (1919) and in the Treaty of Lausanne (1923) the community of nations had recognized that all the Arab territories, including Palestine, of the formerly Ottoman provinces were to have granted to them their freedom as provisionally independent nations.

Despite the historical injustice inflicted on the Palestinian Arab people resulting in their dispersion and depriving them of their right to self-determination, following upon U.N. General Assembly Resolution 181 (1947), which partitioned Palestine into two states, one Arab, one Jewish, yet it is this Resolution that still provides those conditions of international legitimacy that ensure the right of the Palestinian Arab people to sovereignty and national independence.

By stages, the occupation of Palestine and parts of the Arab territories by Israeli forces, the willed dispossession and expulsion from their ancestral homes of the majority of Palestine's civilian inhabitants was achieved by organized terror; those Palestinians who remained, as a vestige subjugated in its homeland, were persecuted and forced to endure the destruction of their national life.

Thus were principles of international legitimacy violated. Thus were the Charter of the United Nations and its resolutions disfigured, for they had recognized the Palestinian Arab people's national rights, including the right of return, the right to independence, the right to sovereignty over territory and homeland.

In Palestine and on its perimeters, in exile distant and near, the Palestinian Arab people never faltered and never abandoned its conviction in its rights of return and independence. Occupation, massacres, and dispersion achieved no political identity, as Palestinians went forward with their destiny, undeterred and unbowed. And from out of the long years of trial in ever mounting struggle, the Palestinian political identity emerged further consolidated and confirmed. And the collective Palestinian National will forged for itself a political embodiment, the Palestine Liberation Organization, its sole legitimate representative, recognized by the world community as a whole, as well as by related regional and international institutions. Standing on the very rock of conviction in the Palestinian people's inalienable rights, and on the ground of Arab national consensus, and of international legitimacy, the P.L.O. led the campaigns of its great people, molded into unity and powerful resolve, one and indivisible in its triumphs, even as it suffered massacres and confinement within and without its home. And so Palestinian resistance was clarified and raised into the forefront of Arab and world awareness, as the struggle of Palestinian Arab people achieved unique prominence among the world's liberation movements in the modern era. The massive national uprising, the "intifada," now intensifying in cumulative scope and power on occupied Palestinian territories, as well as the unflinching resistance of the refugee camps outside the homeland, have elevated consciousness of the Palestinian truth and right into still higher realms of comprehension and actuality. Now at last the curtain has been dropped around a whole epoch of prevarication and negation. The Intifada has set steps to the mind of official Israel, which has for too long rolled exclusively upon myth and terror to deny Palestinian existence altogether. Because of the Intifada and its revolutionary irreversible impulse, the history of Palestine has therefore arrived at a decisive juncture.

Whereas the Palestinian people reaffirms most definitely its inalienable rights in the land of its patrimony:

> Now by virtue of natural, and the exercise of those rights historical and legal right and the sacrifices of successive generations who gave of themselves in defense of the freedom and independence of their homeland;
>
> In pursuance of Resolutions adopted by Arab Summit Conference and relying on the authority bestowed by international legitimacy as embodied in the Resolutions of the United Nations Organization since 1947;
>
> and in exercise by the Palestinian Arab people of its rights to self-determination, political independence, and sovereignty over its territory,
>
> The Palestine National Council, in the name of God, and in the name of the Palestinian Arab people, hereby proclaims the establishment of the state of Palestine on our Palestinian territory with its capital Jerusalem (Al Quds Ash Sharif).

The state of Palestine is the state of Palestinians wherever they may be. The state is for them to enjoy, [exercising] in it their collective national and cultural identity, pursuing in it a complete equality of rights. In it will be safeguarded their political and religious convictions and their human dignity by means of a parliamentary democratic system of governance, itself based on freedom of expression and the freedom to form parties. The rights of minorities will be duly respected by the majority. Governance will be based on principles of social justice, equality, and nondiscrimination in public rights of men or women on grounds of race, religion, color, or sex under the aegis of a constitution that ensures the rule of law and on an independent judiciary. Thus shall these principles allow no departure from

Palestine's age-old spiritual and civilizational heritage of tolerance and religious coexistence.

The state of Palestine is an Arab state, an integral and indivisible part of the Arab nation, at one with the nation in heritage and civilization, with it also in its aspiration for liberation, progress, democracy, and unity. The state of Palestine affirms its obligation to abide by the Charter of the League of Arab States, whereby the coordination of the Arab states with each other shall be strengthened. It calls upon Arab compatriots to consolidate and enhance the emergence in reality of our state, to mobilize potential, and to intensify efforts whose goal is to end Israeli occupation.

The state of Palestine proclaims its commitment to the principles and purposes of the United Nations, and to the Universal Declaration of Human Rights. It proclaims its commitment as well to the principles and policies of the Non-Aligned Movement.

It further announces itself to be a peace-loving state, in adherence to the principles of peaceful coexistence. It will join with all states and peoples in order to assure a permanent peace based upon justice and the respect of rights so that humanity's potential for well-being may be assured, and earnest competition for excellence be maintained, and in which confidence in the future will eliminate fear for those who are just and for whom justice is the only recourse.

In the context of its struggle for peace in the Land of Love and Peace, the state of Palestine calls upon the United Nations to bear special responsibility for the Palestinian Arab people and its homeland. It calls upon all peace- and freedom-loving peoples and states to assist it in the attainment of its objectives, to provide it with security, to alleviate the tragedy of its people, and to help it terminate Israel's occupation of the Palestinian territories.

The state of Palestine herewith declares that it believes in the settlement of regional and international disputes by peaceful means, in accordance with the U.N. Charter and resolutions. Without prejudice to its natural right to defend its territorial integrity and independence, it therefore rejects the threat of use of force, violence, and terrorism against its territorial integrity, or political independence, as it also rejects their use against the territorial integrity of other states.

Therefore, on this day unlike all others, November 15, 1988, as we stand at the threshold of a new dawn, in all honor and modesty we humbly bow to the sacred spirits of our fallen ones, Palestinian and Arab, by the purity of whose sacrifice for the homeland our sky has been illuminated and our land given life. Our hearts are lifted up and irradiated by the light emanating from the much blessed Intifada, from those who have endured and have fought the fight of the camps, of dispersion, of exile, from those who have borne the standard of freedom, our children, our aged, our youth, our prisoners, detainees, and wounded, all those whose ties to our sacred soil are confirmed in camp, village, and town. We render special tribute to that brave Palestinian woman, guardian of sustenance and life, keeper of our people's perennial flame. To the souls of our sainted martyrs, to the whole of our Palestinian Arab people, to all free and honorable peoples everywhere, we pledge that our struggle shall be continued until the occupation ends, and the foundation of our sovereignty and independence shall be fortified accordingly.

Therefore, we call upon our great people to rally to the banner of Palestine, to cherish and defend it, so that it may forever be the symbol of our freedom and dignity in that homeland, which is a homeland for the free, now and always.

*In the name of God, the Compassionate, the Merciful.*

Say:

"O God, Master of the Kingdom, Thou givest the Kingdom to whom Thou will, and seizest the Kingdom from whom Thou will. Thou exaltest whom Thou will, and Thou abases whom Thou will; in Thy hand is the good; Thou art powerful over everything."

SADAGA ALISHU AL-AZIM

## 2. Official Statements by the Leaders of the Christian Communities of Jerusalem from the Beginning of the Intifada to the Peace Conference

*The churches in Palestine, with their headquarters in Jerusalem, could not remain untouched by the situation existing in the occupied territories. Although, based on their history, these churches had had little contact with each other, they were more or less forced during the Intifada to approach each other, cooperate more closely, and jointly speak for justice and peace. The situation under the occupation had become unbearable.*

*The most important proclamations of the churches have been issued in the last five years. They were signed by "the heads of the Christian communities in Jerusalem." Signatures were from the following church representatives: the three patriarchs of the Greek Orthodox, Roman Catholic, and Armenian Orthodox churches, respectively; the custos of the Holy Land; the bishops of Coptic Orthodox, Syrian Orthodox, Ethiopian Orthodox, Greek Catholic, Anglican, and Lutheran churches.*

*The statements were for the most part reactions to particular events in the Holy Land. Most often they were reactions to painful events of a political nature which had forced the churches to take a position. Some of these events were the outbreak of the Intifada; the brutal behavior of the Israeli army toward the Palestinian civilian population; the Israeli occupation of the Greek Orthodox St. John Hospice in the Old City of Jerusalem; the massacre on the grounds of the Al Haram El-Sharif; the Gulf crisis and its consequences; and assaults on Christian clergy, Christian sacred places, and Christian archaeological sites.*

*There are only two proclamations reacting to favorable events: the Declaration of the state of Palestine through the P.L.O., and the start of the Peace Conference.*

*I here reproduce these statements without commentary.*

## 1. STATEMENT ISSUED BY THE HEADS OF THE
## CHRISTIAN COMMUNITIES IN JERUSALEM

*Jerusalem, January 22, 1988*

To all our sons and daughters, our sisters and brothers in the Holy Land.

> "Thus says the LORD: 'Let not the wise man glory in his wisdom, let not the mighty man glory in his might, let not the rich man glory in his riches; but let him who glories glory in this, that he understands and knows me, that I am the LORD who practices kindness, justice, and righteousness in the earth; for in these things I delight,' says the LORD" (Jer 9:23–24).

The recent painful events in our land which have resulted in so many victims, both killed and wounded, are a clear indication of the grievous suffering of our people on the West Bank and in the Gaza Strip. They are also a visible expression of our people's aspirations to achieve their legal rights and the realization of their hopes.

We, the heads of the Christian Communities in Jerusalem, would like to express in all honesty and clarity that we take our stand with truth and justice against all forms of injustice and oppression. We stand with the suffering and the oppressed, we stand with the refugees and the deported, with the distressed and the victims of injustice, we stand with those who mourn and are bereaved, with the hungry and the poor. In accordance with the Word of God through the prophet Isaiah, chapter 1, verse 17: "Learn to do good; seek justice, correct oppression; defend the fatherless, plead for the widow," we call upon the faithful to pray and to labor for justice and peace for all the peoples of our area.

And in response to the same Word of God, prompted by our faith in God and our Christian duty, we have decided to call upon all our sons and daughters who are, with us, an integral part of the people of this Holy Land who are laboring and witnessing for justice and peace, to give expression to what we feel, we ought to do in these ways:

We call upon faithful Christians to dedicate next Friday, 29 January 1988, as a day of fasting and self-denial, identifying ourselves with our brothers and sisters in the camps on the West Bank and in the Gaza Strip.

We request you to give what you thus save toward the support of our needy brothers and sisters, remembering that Friday speaks to us of the passion of our Lord Jesus Christ, of his crucifixion, and of his death to redeem all humanity.

We have resolved to set apart Sunday, 31 January 1988, in all the churches of our various communities as a day of prayer and preaching when fervent prayer will be offered in the regular worship services that justice and peace may be realized in our land, so that all may live there in safety, security and peace. At the end of these services, donations toward the support of our needy brothers and sisters will be collected.

We solemnly charge the Christian faithful to fill the churches by their presence, and actively to contribute to the success of what we intend to do, praying that God may inspire and direct all leaders and people in authority to bring to reality what all of us hope and work for so that the foundations of truth, justice, and peace may be firmly laid in our beloved part of the world.

Therefore, we again state unequivocally that all our Christian churches in this country, standing together, seek real peace based on justice and which will never be established unless every person's rights are fully respected; only when this happens will crises cease, peace permeate our country, and the song of the angels on the birthday of Jesus Christ, "the king of peace," be a reality. "Glory to God in the highest, and on earth peace, good will toward all."


## 2. TO OUR CHRISTIAN SISTERS AND BROTHERS THROUGHOUT THE WORLD

*December 23, 1988*

This is the voice of the Mother Church of Jerusalem.

We, the heads of Christian churches of Jerusalem, reach out to you today while our hearts are burning for peace in this Holy City of Jerusalem and in the entire Holy Land.

The decisions of the Palestine National Council (P.N.C.) in Algeria on November 15, 1988, after twelve months of uprising, are for us a positive step and a sign that a new time is beginning on the road toward justice, reconciliation, and peace.

Peace in this land is not like peace in any other land. It is peace in the land that is holy to all Christians.

Pope John Paul II, in his encyclical *Redemptoris Mater*, in which he announced the Marian year 1987, wrote: "Palestine is the spiritual homeland of all Christians because it is the home of Jesus and Mary."

Peace for the Holy Land therefore has a special spiritual significance. The churches of the entire world cannot be unconcerned about peace in the Holy Land and in the whole Middle East.

Therefore we ask you to work with us for peace:

1. We earnestly beg you, especially the bishops of the various churches, church organizations and bishops' conferences throughout the world, to encourage Palestinians and Israelis, Jews, Christians, and Muslims to move forward in the peace process.

2. On the occasion of the coming feast of Christmas we ask you to make a public statement expressing the complete support and commitment of the Christian world to peace in the Holy Land.

3. We further ask you to communicate this statement of support to your faithful, to your respective governments, and through all available means of the mass media.

May the feast of Christmas, the celebration of the birth of the Prince of Peace in Bethlehem, be the beginning of a new era in the local and international search for justice, reconciliation and peace for Jerusalem, the Holy Land, and all the peoples of the country.

THE HEADS OF CHRISTIAN CHURCHES IN JERUSALEM

## 3. STATEMENT BY THE HEADS OF THE CHRISTIAN COMMUNITIES IN JERUSALEM

*June 1989*

We, the heads of the Christian Communities in the Holy City, have met together in view of the grave situation prevailing in Jerusalem and the whole of our country.

It is our Christian conviction that as spiritual leaders we have an urgent duty to follow up the developments in this situation and to make known to the world the conditions of life of our people here in the Holy Land.

In Jerusalem, on the West Bank, and in Gaza our people experience in their daily lives constant deprivation of their fundamental rights because of arbitrary actions deliberately taken by the authorities. Our people are often subjected to unprovoked harassment and hardship.

We are particularly concerned by the tragic and unnecessary loss of Palestinian lives, especially among minors. Unarmed and innocent people are being killed by the unwarranted use of firearms, and hundreds are wounded by the excessive use of force.

We protest against the frequent shooting incidents in the vicinity of holy places.

We also condemn the practice of mass administrative arrests, and of continuing detention of adults and minors without trial.

We further condemn the use of all forms of collective punishment, including the demolition of homes and depriving whole communities of basic services such as water and electricity.

We appeal to the world community to support our demand for the reopening of schools and universities, closed for the past sixteen months, so that thousands of our children can enjoy again their basic right to education.

We demand that the authorities respect the right of believers to enjoy free access to all places of worship on the holy days of all religions.

We affirm our human solidarity and sympathy with all who are suffering and oppressed; we pray for the return of peace based on justice to Jerusalem and the Holy Land; and we request the international community and the United Nations Organization to give urgent attention to the plight of the Palestinian people, and to work for a speedy and just resolution of the Palestinian problem.

*Signed by the Greek Orthodox Patriarch; Latin Patriarch; Armenian Patriarch; Custos of the Holy Land; Coptic Archbishop; Syrian Archbishop; Anglican Bishop; Lutheran Bishop.*

## 4. STATEMENT OF THE HEADS OF THE CHRISTIAN CHURCHES AND COMMUNITIES IN JERUSALEM

*April 23, 1990*

Today, Monday, April 23, 1990, we, the patriarchs, the Custos, the heads of the Christian churches and communities in Jerusalem, have gathered together to consider our response to the extremely grave events that occurred during Holy Week and their enduring consequences.

In the afternoon of April 11, 1990, Wednesday in Holy Week, 150 settlers, many of them armed men, forcibly occupied St. John's Hospice in the heart of the Christian quarter of the Old City, a 3000-square-meter property of the Greek Orthodox Patriarchate.

Their action received support from Israeli authorities. It was financed, at least in great part, by the government, and there have been visits by government ministers and parliamentary authorities to encourage the settlers. Subsequently, it appears that high-level governmental authorities intervened to restrain the police from carrying out judicial eviction orders.

This action occurred toward the culmination of Holy Week and caused grievous disruption to some of the most solemn rites of the Christian religion, at the holiest shrine of Christendom, the Basilica of the Holy Sepulcher Church.

This government-backed settlers' action continues to provoke almost daily violent incidents in and around the area containing the Holy Sepulcher and the centers of church governance, and has occasioned the provocative presence of numerous armed men in the same restricted area. Consequently, freedom of access to the Holy Sepulcher and freedom of worship within it have been threatened.

This act of armed settlement seriously jeopardizes the integrity and the cultural and religious autonomy of the Christian, Armenian, and Muslim quarters, in violation of the centuries-old status and character of these quarters of the Holy City, honored by all previous rulers of Jerusalem, and the international community (and which the Israeli government authorities have repeatedly pledged themselves to uphold).

This action further endangers the survival of all Christian communities in the Holy City.

We, the heads of Jerusalem's Christian churches and communities unreservedly condemn the actions of the settlers.

We deplore the open support and encouragement they have received from Israeli government quarters.

We demand that the Israeli authorities effect the immediate removal of these settlers and secure the property for its legitimate owners, the Greek Orthodox Patriarchate.

We appeal to the international community, to all churches and religious leaders, and to all people of goodwill throughout the world to give their active support to our call.

We have unanimously decided that:

(i) On Friday, April 27, all Christian holy places in Jerusalem, Nazareth, and Bethlehem and elsewhere in the Holy Land will close their doors as of 9:00 A.M. and will not reopen until the following day.

(ii) On the same day, all church bells throughout the country will ring a funeral toll every hour on the hour from 9:00 A.M. until noon.

(iii) Sunday, April 29, shall be a special day of prayer on behalf of the Christian community of Jerusalem, in which we invite all our fellow Christian believers throughout the world to join.

We have decided to remain in an open session to monitor developments in the case.

*Jerusalem, April 23, 1990*

*Signed by the Greek Orthodox Patriarch of Jerusalem, Latin Patriarch of Jerusalem, Armenian Patriarch of Jerusalem, Custos of the Holy Land, Coptic Archbishop of Jerusalem, Syrian Archbishop of Jerusalem, Ethiopian Archbishop of Jerusalem, Anglican Bishop in Jerusalem and Presiding Bishop of the Anglican Church, Greek-Catholic Patriarchal Vicar, the Lutheran Propst of Jerusalem, Lutheran Bishop of Jerusalem.*

## 5. STATEMENT

*October 1990*

We, the Christian communities of Jerusalem share deeply the sorrow and the sufferings of our people after the tragic events during which tens of people were killed and scores wounded on Monday, 8 October, 1990, at 11:00 A.M. in the venue of Al-Haram El Sharif and the Wailing Wall.

We cannot but condemn this massacre, and we do point out that it should not be allowed to create provocative atmospheres that lead to conflict and confrontation among the adherents of the three monotheistic religions.

We extend our condolences to the families of the victims and pray to God that all reasons for conflict may soon come to an end and that truth, justice, and peace may prevail.

*Signed by the Greek Orthodox Patriarchate of Jerusalem, Latin Patriarchate of Jerusalem, Armenian Patriarchate of Jerusalem, Custos of the Holy Land, Syrian Orthodox Church, Greek Catholic Church, Anglican Bishop RIC, Lutheran Bishop RIC.*

## 6. CHRISTMAS MESSAGE AND STATEMENT BY THE PATRIARCHS AND HEADS OF THE CHURCHES IN THE HOLY LAND

*December 20, 1990*

We, the patriarchs and the heads of the Christian churches in Jerusalem, have met today, when our region is living through one of its most crucial crises in its modern history, dangerously poised on the brink of war.

We the spiritual heads of the Christian communities in the Holy Land, call upon the world's leaders to follow the course of negotiation and peace and spare the region from devastating destruction.

We deplore the fact that the patriarchs and the heads of the Christian churches in the Holy Land are constant targets of attacks by Israeli officials and the Israeli media. We consider it our sacred duty to voice our concern about human rights violations in the Occupied Territories. We maintain fraternal relations with Muslims in the Occupied Territories, as well as with Jews in Israel. We call upon all people to reconcile, forgive, and love each other. We call upon the responsible parties to follow the path of negotiation rather than violence.

The prospects for constructive dialogue and peace in the Holy Land are receding. Despair is the pervasive mood.

We are witnessing a deterioration in the condition of the Palestinian people. There is considerable suffering and loss of life. We pray for a quick reconciliation and a just settlement of the conflict.

As we look back over the past year, we witness that the local church had to cope with a host of problems of a new nature:

Constant attempts to change the demographic character of the Old City of Jerusalem, for example, the forcible and continuing seizure by "Ateret Cohanim" settlers of the St. John's Hospice (property of the Greek Orthodox Patriarchate).

Continuing erosion of the traditional rights and centuries-old privileges of the churches. Municipal and state taxes are being imposed on the churches, in addition to encroachment on church land and properties, thus endangering their very survival.

We express our deep concern over the new problems confronting the local church. They interfere with the proper functioning of our religious institutions, and we call upon the civil authorities in the country to safeguard our historic rights and status honored by all governments.

We ask our sons and daughters to join us in fervent prayer on Christmas Day, that the Lord may grant us patience, love, and strength.

In view of the continuing sad state of affairs in our land, we have decided to restrict Christmas festivities to religious ceremonies, without any manifestation of jubilation, and to devote our prayers to the peace of the land and the world. Furthermore all exchange visits between the communities are cancelled.

Once more, we launch an urgent appeal from Bethlehem, to all peace-loving people to influence their leaders so that they may resolve the conflict in the Gulf without bloodshed and its inevitable loss of human lives.

We pray to the Lord to guide the leaders of the world along the path of peace and justice, and we pray for a year free of the threat of war and violence, and extend our blessings to all the faithful.

*Signed by the Greek Orthodox Patriarch of Jerusalem, Latin Patriarch of Jerusalem, Armenian Patriarch of Jerusalem, Custos of the Holy Land, Syrian Archbishop of Jerusalem, Anglican Bishop in Jerusalem and Presiding Bishop of the Anglican Church, Greek-Catholic Patriarchal Vicar, Lutheran Bishop of Jerusalem.*

## 7. EASTER MESSAGE OF THE PATRIARCHS AND THE HEADS OF THE CHURCHES OF THE HOLY LAND

*March 23, 1991*

As we celebrate the Resurrection of our Lord, we, the patriarchs and the heads of the Christian churches in the Holy Land share with you, our beloved children, the message of joy and hope in the risen Christ.

We have gathered to reflect on the events of the last months and the future of our region.

We have repeatedly expressed our opposition to war, violence, and the use of force as means to resolve conflicts and misunderstanding between nations.

We were deeply pained to witness a destructive war which took a heavy toll in human lives.

During the whole duration of the war, the Occupied Territories were subjected to an unwarranted harsh curfew causing considerable economic stress and human hardship. As a result, the population of the West Bank and Gaza are now in dire need of massive international financial support.

To date, despite local and international protest, it is more than forty months that universities in the West Bank and Gaza remain closed. This has adversely affected the education of our youth, depriving them of one of their most basic rights. We call upon the Israeli authorities to honor their commitment to free and unrestricted education.

The Christian churches of the Holy Land, throughout their long historical presence, and despite many vicissitudes, have managed to retain their historical rights in the service of their faithful and the holy places. Today the churches face many difficulties maintaining these rights. We stress again that our historical rights are not negotiable. The ongoing occupation of St. John's Hospice (adjoining the Holy Sepulcher) by Jewish settlers is a primary source of our concern. In this occupation we see an attempt to change the unique and pluralistic character of Jerusalem. We demand the authorities to honor their commitments to the churches.

We are confident that the international community, after the Gulf crisis and war, is able to find a just solution to the Palestinian-Israeli conflict. A just solution would end the cycle of violence and injustice.

During this Holy Week we call upon you, dear faithful, and upon the whole world to pray fervently for the just solution of the Palestinian, Lebanese and Cypriot problems. Let us pray for the recovery of peace, prosperity, and stability in our Holy Land.

Lasting peace is only possible through coexistence, reconciliation, and the fulfillment of the aspirations of all peoples by the attainment of their full sovereignty.

May the risen Christ, who reconciled God with humanity through his crucifixion, grant us in this Holy Week wisdom, strength, and inspiration for the reconciliation of all people, as children of the same heavenly Father and Creator of the universe.

We ask you, dear faithful, to pray in this spirit, especially during the Holy Week. May the resurrected Christ bestow his blessings upon our land and grant us lasting and just peace.

*Signed by the Greek Orthodox Patriarch of Jerusalem, Latin Patriarch of Jerusalem, Armenian Patriarch of Jerusalem, Custos of the Holy Land, Coptic Archbishop of Jerusalem, Syrian Archbishop of Jerusalem, Anglican Bishop in Jerusalem and Presiding Bishop of the Anglican Church, the Greek-Catholic Patriarchal Vicar, Lutheran Bishop of Jerusalem.*

## 8. STATEMENT BY THE HEADS OF THE CHURCHES IN THE HOLY LAND

*May 30, 1991*

We express our deep concern and alarm over the growing feeling of insecurity and fear among our people and Churches.

Last week, because of a misleading and tendentious dissemination of facts, the Franciscans were subjected to calumnious reporting in the Israeli media. We were equally shocked to witness an organized demonstration, during which a Jewish extremist group burned the Vatican flag and marched freely and unimpeded with hostile and anti-Christian slogans against one of our convents in Jerusalem, St. Saviour's, the main Monastery of the Custody of the Holy Land.

The occupation of the St. John's Hospice of the Greek Orthodox Patriarchate by another Jewish extremist group during Holy Week of April 1990, was another serious and unprecedented encroachment on Christian rights and property in the history of the Holy City.

Such grave incidents constitute a serious threat to the future of Christianity and its rights in the Holy Land.

We call upon the responsible authorities to honor the historical inviolability and integrity of the holy places, churches, and convents in the Holy City. No one has the right to exploit the holy places for political and repressive reasons. No one has the right to enter churches or convents without the authorization of their legitimate owners and superiors. We denounce the distortion of facts as they appeared in the *Jerusalem Post* on Tuesday, May 28, 1991.

May Almighty God inspire all the responsible leaders in this conflict to strive for peace and justice and guide their people by all available means, including the media, toward peace, reconciliation, and elimination of the underlying causes of social and political injustice and turmoil.

*Signed by the Greek Orthodox Patriarch of Jerusalem, Latin Patriarch of Jerusalem, Armenian Patriarch of Jerusalem, Custos of the Holy Land, Syrian Archbishop of Jerusalem, Anglican Bishop in Jerusalem and Presiding Bishop of the Anglican Church, Greek-Catholic Patriarchal Vicar, Lutheran Bishop of Jerusalem.*

## 9. MESSAGE TO THE DELEGATES OF THE PEACE CONFERENCE IN MADRID FROM THE PATRIARCHS AND THE HEADS OF THE CHRISTIAN COMMUNITIES IN JERUSALEM

*October 30, 1991*

*"Blessed are the peace seekers,
for they shall be called children of God."*

On this historic occasion, we the patriarchs and the heads of the churches in Jerusalem greet you in the name of the God of peace. From this Holy City we raise our prayers for all those who have worked tirelessly so that a new foundation for peace can be built. We pray as you begin your deliberations in Madrid that the spirit of reconciliation and understanding will prevail and that justice and peace will come to our tormented land.

We all face the challenge to be peacemakers. We repeat our deep commitment and pastoral concern for the welfare of all peoples in this land. As patriarchs and heads of the Christian communities in Jerusalem with a continuous presence of two millennia in the Holy Land, and being entrusted by the universal church to safeguard the holy places of Christianity, we call upon all parties concerned to remember that all people carry the same image and likeness of God and are children of the same Lord. We call upon you to persevere in your deliberations for the peoples of the Middle East.

We assure you of our constant prayers. On this very day as you meet in Madrid, thousands of Christians in the Holy Land as well as throughout the world are praying fervently for the success of the peace conference. We pray that you will be guided to lay the foundation for a peaceful resolution of the Middle East conflict based on justice and truth for all. We pray that all the people and countries of our region will be able to live in security, freedom, and dignity. We pray that the human and political rights of all will be guarded and democratic principles honored.

May the God of justice and peace guide you in all endeavors.

*Signed by the Greek Orthodox Patriarch of Jerusalem, Latin Patriarch of Jerusalem, Armenian Patriarch of Jerusalem, Custos of the Holy Land, Syrian Archbishop of Jerusalem, Anglican Bishop in Jerusalem and Presiding Bishop of the Anglican Church, Greek-Catholic Patriarchal Vicar.*

## 10. STATEMENT BY THE HEADS OF THE CHURCHES IN THE HOLY LAND

*January 14, 1992*

As we stand upon the threshold of a New Year we, the patriarchs and heads of the Christian churches in Jerusalem, look ahead to a period of peace and justice in which our children may grow and prosper, unencumbered by fears and uncertainties, strong in their faith in the Lord.

It is our heartfelt wish and hope to see this blessed land endowed with peace and to see justice prevail across its breadth and length.

We address this longing to the authorities in Israel, to the Palestinian leaders, and to the Palestinian and Jewish peoples; and we beseech the Lord to give us all light and strength to effect reconciliation and find peace, justice, and security for all.

But certain untoward developments that occurred recently and that continue to occur to this day, threaten to thwart the fulfillment of this longing.

We are profoundly concerned over several grave incidents besetting our life and that of our communities, and causing tribulation not only among the local Christian population but among our brethren in all parts of the world as well.

One of the most serious incidents, and the one with the widest repercussions, has been the seizure of houses in Silwan by settlers who enjoy public funding and seek to evict many other families from the same neighborhood of Silwan.

Since April 1990, the St. John's Hospice, adjoining the Holy Sepulcher, has been occupied by settlers. Despite official statements that the building is to be restored to its original legitimate owners, the Greek Orthodox Patriarchate, it is still occupied by the settlers.

Furthermore, in recent months Ateret Cohanim has begun intensifying its aggressive settlement policy in and around Jerusalem. Unfortunately, the Israeli authorities, though fully aware of the implications, have adopted an ambivalent attitude to the depredations of the settlers.

We pray to the Almighty that peace and understanding may reign in our region, and that his Holy Land may be blessed with stability and prosperity.

We call upon all the faithful to pray that the Lord may bestow upon us the grace of peace in the coming year.

*Signed by the Greek Orthodox Patriarch of Jerusalem, Latin Patriarch of Jerusalem, Armenian Patriarch of Jerusalem, Custos of the Holy Land, Syrian Archbishop of Jerusalem, Anglican Bishop in Jerusalem and Presiding Bishop of the Anglican Church, Greek-Catholic Patriarchal Vicar, Lutheran Bishop of Jerusalem.*

# 3. Agreement on the Gaza Strip and the Jericho Area

The Government of the State of Israel and the Palestine Liberation Organization (hereinafter "the P.L.O."), the representative of the Palestinian people;

## Preamble

WITHIN the framework of the Middle East peace process initiated at Madrid in October 1991;

REAFFIRMING their determination to live in peaceful coexistence, mutual dignity and security, while recognizing their mutual legitimate and political rights;

REAFFIRMING their desire to achieve a just, lasting and comprehensive peace settlement through the agreed political process;

REAFFIRMING their adherence to the mutual recognition and commitments expressed in the letters dated September 9, 1993, signed by and exchanged between the Prime Minister of Israel and the Chairman of the P.L.O.;

REAFFIRMING their understanding that the interim self-government arrangements, including the arrangements to apply in the Gaza Strip and the Jericho Area contained in this Agreement, are an integral part of the whole peace process and that the negotiations on the permanent status will lead to the implementation of Security Council Resolutions 242 and 338;

DESIROUS of putting into effect the Declaration of Principles on Interim Self-Government Arrangements signed in Washington, D.C. on September 13, 1993, and the Agreed Minutes thereto (hereinafter "the Declaration of Principles"), and in particular the Protocol on withdrawal of Israeli forces from the Gaza Strip and the Jericho Area;

HEREBY AGREE to the following arrangements regarding the Gaza Strip and the Jericho Area:

## Article I
DEFINITIONS

For the purpose of this Agreement:

**a.** the Gaza Strip and the Jericho Area are delineated on map Nos. 1 and 2 not attached to this Agreement [not reproduced here];

**b.** "the Settlements" means the Gush Katif and Erez settlement areas, as well as the other settlements in the Gaza Strip, as shown on attached map No. 1;

**c.** "the Military Installation Area" means the Israeli military installation area along the Egyptian border in the Gaza Strip as shown on map No. 1; and

**d.** the term "Israelis" shall also include Israeli statutory agencies and corporations registered in Israel.

## Article II
SCHEDULED WITHDRAWAL OF ISRAELI MILITARY FORCES

**1.** Israel shall implement an accelerated and scheduled withdrawal of Israeli military forces from the Gaza Strip and from the Jericho Area to begin immediately with the signing of this Agreement. Israel shall complete such withdrawal within three weeks from this date.

**2.** Subject to the arrangements included in the Protocol Concerning Withdrawal of Israeli Military Forces and Security Arrangements attached as Annex I, the Israeli withdrawal shall include evacuating all military bases and other fixed installations to be handed over to the Palestinian Police, to be established pursuant to Article IX below (hereinafter "the Palestinian Police").

**3.** In order to carry out Israel's responsibility for external security and for internal security and public order of Settlements and Israelis, Israel shall, concurrently with the withdrawal, redeploy its remaining military forces to the Settlements and the Military Installation Area, in accordance with the provisions of this Agreement. Subject to the provisions of the Agreement, this redeployment shall constitute full implementation of Article XIII of the Declaration of Principles with regard to the Gaza Strip and the Jericho Area only.

**4.** For the purposes of this Agreement, "Israeli military forces" may include Israel police and other Israeli security forces.

**5.** Israelis, including Israeli military forces, may continue to use roads freely within the Gaza Strip and the Jericho Area. Palestinians may use public roads crossing the Settlements freely, as provided for in Annex I.

**6.** The Palestinian Police shall be deployed and shall assume responsibility for public order and internal security of Palestinians in accordance with this Agreement and Annex I.

## Article III
TRANSFER OF AUTHORITY

**1.** Israel shall transfer authority as specified in this Agreement from the Israeli military government and its Civil Administration to the Palestinian Authority, hereby established, in accordance with Article V of this Agreement, except for the authority that Israel shall continue to exercise as specified in this Agreement.

**2.** As regards the transfer and assumption of authority in civil spheres, powers and responsibilities shall be transferred and assumed as set out in the Protocol Concerning Civil Affairs attached as Annex II.

**3.** Arrangements for a smooth and peaceful transfer of the agreed powers and responsibilities are set out in Annex II.

**4.** Upon the completion of the Israeli withdrawal and the transfer of powers and responsibilities as detailed in paragraphs 1 and 2 above and in Annex II, the Civil Administration in the Gaza Strip and the Jericho Area will be dissolved and the Israeli military government will be withdrawn.

The withdrawal of the military government shall not prevent it from continuing to exercise the powers and responsibilities specified in this Agreement.

**5.** A Joint Civil Affairs Coordination and Cooperation Committee (hereinafter "the CAC") and two Joint Regional Civil Affairs Subcommittees for the Gaza Strip and the Jericho Area respectively shall be established in order to provide for coordination and cooperation in civil affairs between the Palestinian Authority and Israel, as detailed in Annex II.

**6.** The offices of the Palestinian Authority shall be located in the Gaza Strip and the Jericho Area pending the inauguration of the Council to be elected pursuant to the Declaration of Principles.

## Article IV
STRUCTURE AND COMPOSITION OF THE PALESTINIAN AUTHORITY

**1.** The Palestinian Authority will consist of one body of 24 members which shall carry out and be responsible for all the legislative and executive powers and responsibilities transferred to it under this Agreement, in accordance with this Article, and shall be responsible for the exercise of judicial functions in accordance with Article VI, subparagraph 1.b of this Agreement.

**2.** The Palestinian Authority shall administer the departments transferred to it and may establish, within its jurisdiction, other departments and subordinate administrative units as necessary for the fulfillment of its responsibilities. It shall determine its own internal procedures.

**3.** The PLO shall inform the Government of Israel of the names of the members of the Palestinian Authority and any change of members. Changes in the membership of the Palestinian Authority will take effect upon an exchange of letters between the PLO and the Government of Israel.

**4.** Each member of the Palestinian Authority shall enter into office upon undertaking to act in accordance with this Agreement.

## Article V
JURISDICTION

**1.** The authority of the Palestinian Authority encompasses all matters that fall within its territorial, functional and personal jurisdiction, as follows:

**a.** The territorial jurisdiction covers the Gaza Strip and the Jericho Area territory, as defined in Article I, except for Settlements and the Military Installation Area.

Territorial jurisdiction shall include land, subsoil and territorial waters, in accordance with the provisions of this Agreement.

**b.** The functional jurisdiction encompasses all powers and responsibilities as specified in this Agreement. This jurisdiction does not include foreign relations, internal security and public order of Settlements and the Military Installation Area and Israelis, and external security.

**c.** The personal jurisdiction extends to all persons within the territorial jurisdiction referred to above, except for Israelis, unless otherwise provided in this Agreement.

**2.** The Palestinian Authority has, within its authority, legislative, executive and judicial powers and responsibilities, as provided for in this Agreement.

**3. a.** Israel has authority over the Settlements, the Military Installation Area, Israelis, external security, internal security and public order of Settlements, the Military Installation Area and Israelis, and those agreed powers and responsibilities specified in this Agreement.

**b.** Israel shall exercise its authority through its military government, which, for that end, shall continue to have the necessary legislative, judicial and executive powers and responsibilities, in accordance with international law. This provision shall not derogate from Israel's applicable legislation over Israelis in personam.

**4.** The exercise of authority with regard to the electromagnetic sphere and airspace shall be in accordance with the provisions of this Agreement.

**5.** The provisions of this Article are subject to the specific legal arrangements detailed in the Protocol Concerning Legal Matters attached as Annex III. Israel and the Palestinian Authority may negotiate further legal arrangements.

**6.** Israel and the Palestinian Authority shall cooperate on matters of legal assistance in criminal and civil matters through the legal subcommittee of the CAC.

## Article VI
POWERS AND RESPONSIBILITIES OF THE PALESTINIAN AUTHORITY

**1.** Subject to the provisions of this Agreement, the Palestinian Authority, within its jurisdiction:

**a.** has legislative powers as set out in Article VII of this Agreement, as well as executive powers;

**b.** will administer justice through an independent judiciary;

**c.** will have, inter alia, power to formulate policies, supervise their implementation, employ staff, establish departments, authorities and institutions, sue and be sued and conclude contracts; and

**d.** will have, inter alia, the power to keep and administer registers and records of the population, and issue certificates, licenses and documents.

**2. a.** In accordance with the Declaration of Principles, the Palestinian Authority will not have powers and responsibilities in the sphere of foreign relations, which sphere includes the establishment abroad of embassies, consulates or other types of foreign missions and posts or permitting their establishment in the Gaza Strip or the Jericho Area, the appointment of or admission of diplomatic and consular staff, and the exercise of diplomatic functions.

**b.** Notwithstanding the provisions of this paragraph, the P.L.O. may conduct negotiations and sign agreements with states or international organizations for the benefit of the Palestinian Authority in the following cases only:

**(1)** economic agreements, as specifically provided in Annex IV of this Agreement;

**(2)** agreements with donor countries for the purpose of implementing arrangements for the provision of assistance to the Palestinian Authority;

**(3)** agreements for the purpose of implementing the regional development plans detailed in Annex IV of the Declaration of Principles or in agreements entered into in the framework of the multilateral negotiations; and

(4) cultural, scientific and educational agreements.

**c.** Dealings between the Palestinian Authority and representatives of foreign states and international organizations, as well as the establishment in the Gaza Strip and the Jericho Area of representative offices other than those described in subparagraph 2.a. above, for the purpose of implementing the agreements referred to in subparagraph 2.b. above, shall not be considered foreign relations.

## Article VII
### LEGISLATIVE POWERS OF THE PALESTINIAN AUTHORITY

**1.** The Palestinian Authority will have the power, within its jurisdiction, to promulgate legislation, including basic laws, laws, regulations and other legislative acts.

**2.** Legislation promulgated by the Palestinian Authority shall be consistent with the provision of this Agreement.

**3.** Legislation promulgated by the Palestinian Authority shall be communicated to a legislation subcommittee to be established by the CAC (hereinafter "the Legislation Subcommittee"). During a period of 30 days from the communication of the legislation, Israel may request that the Legislation Subcommittee decide whether such legislation exceeds the jurisdiction of the Palestinian Authority or is otherwise inconsistent with the provisions of this Agreement.

**4.** Upon receipt of the Israeli request, the Legislation Subcommittee shall decide, as an initial matter, on the entry into force of the legislation pending its decision on the merits of the matter.

**5.** If the Legislation Subcommittee is unable to reach a decision with regard to the entry into force of the legislation within 15 days, this issue will be referred to a board of review. This board of review shall be comprised of two judges, retired judges or senior jurists (hereinafter "Judges"), one from each side, to be appointed from a compiled list of three Judges proposed by each.

In order to expedite the proceedings before this board of review, the two most senior Judges, one from each side, shall develop written informal rules of procedure.

**6.** Legislation referred to the board of review shall enter into force only if the board of review decides that it does not deal with a security issue which falls under Israel's responsibility, that it does not seriously threaten other significant Israeli interests protected by this Agreement and that the entry into force of the legislation could not cause irreparable damage or harm.

**7.** The Legislation Subcommittee shall attempt to reach a decision on the merits of the matter within 30 days from the date of the Israeli request. If this Subcommittee is unable to reach such a decision within this period of 30 days, the matter shall be referred to the Joint Israeli-Palestinian Liaison Committee referred to in Article XV below (hereinafter "Liaison Committee"). This Liaison Committee will deal with the matter immediately and will attempt to settle it within 30 days.

**8.** Where the legislation has not entered into force pursuant to paragraphs 5 or 7 above, this situation shall be maintained pending the decision of the Liaison Committee on the merits of the matter, unless it has decided otherwise.

**9.** Laws and military orders in effect in the Gaza Strip or the Jericho Area prior to the signing of this Agreement shall remain in force, unless amended or abrogated in accordance with this Agreement.

## Article VIII
ARRANGEMENTS FOR SECURITY AND PUBLIC ORDER

**1.** In order to guarantee public order and internal security for the Palestinians of the Gaza Strip and the Jericho Area, the Palestinian Authority shall establish a strong police force, as set out in Article IX below. Israel shall continue to carry the responsibility for defense against external threats, including the responsibility for protecting the Egyptian border and the Jordanian line, and for defense against external threats from the sea and from the air, as well as the responsibility for overall security of Israelis and Settlements, for the purpose of safeguarding their internal security and public order, and will have all the powers to take the steps necessary to meet this responsibility.

**2.** Agreed security arrangements and coordination mechanisms are specified in Annex I.

**3.** A joint Coordination and Cooperation Committee for mutual security purposes (hereinafter "the JSC"), as well as three joint District Coordination and Cooperation Offices for the Gaza district, the Khan Yunis district and the Jericho district respectively (hereinafter "the DCOs") are hereby established as provided for in Annex I.

**4.** The security arrangements provided for in this Agreement and in Annex I may be reviewed at the request of either Party and may be amended by mutual agreement of the Parties. Specific review arrangements are included in Annex I.

## Article IX
THE PALESTINIAN DIRECTORATE OF POLICE FORCE

**1.** The Palestinian Authority shall establish a strong police force, the Palestinian Directorate of Police Force (hereinafter "the Palestinian Police"). The duties, functions, structure, deployment and composition of the Palestinian Police, together with provisions regarding its equipment and operation, are set out in Annex I, Article III. Rules of conduct governing the activities of the Palestinian Police are set out in Annex I, Article VIII.

**2.** Except for the Palestinian Police referred to in this Article and the Israeli military forces, no other armed forces shall be established or operate in the Gaza Strip or the Jericho Area.

**3.** Except for the arms, ammunition and equipment of the Palestinian Police described in Annex I, Article III, and those of the Israeli military forces, no organization or individual in the Gaza Strip and the Jericho Area shall manufacture, sell, acquire, possess, import or otherwise introduce into the Gaza Strip or the Jericho Area any firearms, ammunition, weapons, explosives, gunpowder or any related equipment, unless otherwise provided for in Annex I.

## Article X
PASSAGES

Arrangements for coordination between Israel and the Palestinian Authority regarding the Gaza-Egypt and Jericho-Jordan passages, as well as any other agreed international crossings, are set out in Annex I, Article X.

## Article XI
SAFE PASSAGE BETWEEN THE GAZA STRIP AND THE JERICHO AREA

Arrangements for safe passage of persons and transportation between the Gaza Strip and Jericho Area are set out in Annex I, Article IX.

## Article XII
RELATIONS BETWEEN ISRAEL AND THE PALESTINIAN AUTHORITY

**1.** Israel and the Palestinian Authority shall seek to foster mutual understanding and tolerance and shall accordingly abstain from incitement, including hostile propaganda, against each other and, without derogating from the principle of freedom of expression, shall take legal measures to prevent such incitement by any organizations, groups or individuals within their jurisdiction.

**2.** Without derogating from the other provisions of this Agreement, Israel and the Palestinian Authority shall cooperate in combatting criminal activity which may affect both sides, including offenses related to trafficking in illegal drugs and psychotropic substances, smuggling, and offenses against property, including offenses related to vehicles.

## Article XIII
ECONOMIC RELATIONS

The economic relations between the two sides are set out in the Protocol on Economic Relations signed in Paris on April 29, 1994, and the Appendices thereto, certified copies of which are attached as Annex IV, and will be governed by the relevant provisions of this Agreement and its Annexes.

## Article XIV
HUMAN RIGHTS AND THE RULE OF LAW

Israel and the Palestinian Authority shall exercise their powers and responsibilities pursuant to this Agreement with due regard to internationally-accepted norms and principles of human rights and the rule of law.

## Article XV
THE JOINT ISRAELI-PALESTINIAN LIAISON COMMITTEE

**1.** The Liaison Committee established pursuant to Article X of the Declaration of Principles shall ensure the smooth implementation of this Agreement.
It shall deal with issues requiring coordination, other issues of common interest and disputes.

**2.** The Liaison Committee shall be composed of an equal number of members from each Party. It may add other technicians and experts as necessary.

**3.** The Liaison Committee shall adopt its rules of procedure, including the frequency and place or places of its meetings.

**4.** The Liaison Committee shall reach its decisions by Agreement.

## Article XVI
LIAISON AND COOPERATION WITH JORDAN EGYPT

**1.** Pursuant to Article XII of the Declaration of Principles, the two Parties shall invite the Governments of Jordan and Egypt to participate in establishing further liaison and cooperation arrangements between the Government of Israel and the Palestinian representatives on the one hand, and the Governments of Jordan and Egypt on the other hand, to promote cooperation between them. These arrangements shall include the constitution of a Continuing Committee.

**2.** The Continuing Committee shall decide by agreement on the modalities of admission of persons displaced from the West Bank and the Gaza Strip in 1967, together with necessary measures to prevent disruption and disorder.

**3.** The Continuing Committee shall deal with other matters of common concern.

## Article XVII
SETTLEMENT OF DIFFERENCES AND DISPUTES

Any differences relating to the application of this Agreement shall be referred to the appropriate coordination and cooperation mechanism established under this Agreement. The provisions of Article XV of the Declaration of Principles shall apply to any such difference which is not settled through the appropriate coordination and cooperation mechanism, namely:

**1.** Disputes arising out of the application or interpretation of this Agreement or any subsequent agreements pertaining to the interim period shall be settled by negotiations through the Liaison Committee.

**2.** Disputes which cannot be settled by negotiations may be settled by a mechanism of conciliation to be agreed between the Parties.

**3.** The Parties may agree to submit to arbitration disputes relating to the interim period, which cannot be settled through conciliation. To this end, upon the agreement of both Parties, the Parties will establish an Arbitration Committee.

## Article XVIII
PREVENTION OF HOSTILE ACTS

Both sides shall take all measures necessary in order to prevent acts of terrorism, crime and hostilities directed against each other, against individuals falling under the other's authority and against their property, and shall take legal measures against offenders. In addition, the Palestinian side shall take all measures necessary to prevent such hostile acts directed against the Settlements, the infrastructure serving them and the Military Installation Area, and the Israeli side shall take all measures necessary to prevent such hostile acts emanating from the Settlements and directed against Palestinians.

## Article XIX
### MISSING PERSONS

The Palestinian Authority shall cooperate with Israel by providing all necessary assistance in the conduct of searches by Israel within the Gaza Strip and the Jericho Area for missing Israelis, as well as by providing information about missing Israelis. Israel shall cooperate with the Palestinian Authority in searching for, and providing necessary information about, missing Palestinians.

## Article XX
### CONFIDENCE BUILDING MEASURES

With a view to creating a positive and supportive public atmosphere to accompany the implementation of this Agreement, and to establish a solid basis of mutual trust and good faith, both Parties agree to carry out confidence building measures as detailed herewith: 1. Upon the signing of this Agreement, Israel will release, or turn over, to the Palestinian Authority within a period of 5 weeks, about 5,000 Palestinians detainees and prisoners, residents of the West Bank and the Gaza Strip. Those released will be free to return to their homes anywhere in the West Bank or the Gaza Strip. Prisoners turned over to the Palestinian Authority shall be obliged to remain in the Gaza Strip or the Jericho Area for the remainder of their sentence.

**2.** After the signing of this Agreement, the two Parties shall continue to negotiate the release of additional Palestinian prisoners and detainees, building on agreed principles.

**3.** The implementation of the above measures will be subject to the fulfillment of the procedures determined by Israeli law for the release and transfer of detainees and prisoners.

**4.** With the assumption of Palestinian authority, the Palestinian side commits itself to solving the problem of those Palestinians who were in contact with the Israeli authorities. Until an agreed solution is found, the Palestinian side undertakes not to prosecute these Palestinians or to harm them in any way.

**5.** Palestinians from abroad whose entry into the Gaza Strip and the Jericho Area is approved pursuant to this Agreement, and to whom the provisions of this

Article are applicable, will not be prosecuted for offenses committed prior to September 13, 1993.

## Article XXI
TEMPORARY INTERNATIONAL PRESENCE

**1.** The Parties agree to a temporary international or foreign presence in the Gaza Strip and the Jericho Area (hereinafter "the TIP"), in accordance with the provisions of this Article.

**2.** The TIP shall consist of 400 qualified personnel, including observers, instructors and other experts, from 5 or 6 of the donor countries.

**3.** The two Parties shall request the donor countries to establish a special fund to provide finance for the TIP.

**4.** The TIP will function for a period of 6 months. The TIP may extend this period, or change the scope of its operation, with the agreement of the two Parties.

**5.** The TIP shall be stationed and operate within the following cities and villages: Gaza, Khan Yunis, Rafah, Deir El Ballah, Jabaliya, Absan, Beit Hanun and Jericho.

**6.** Israel and the Palestinian Authority shall agree on a special Protocol to implement this Article, with the goal of concluding negotiations with the donor countries contributing personnel within two months.

## Article XXII
RIGHTS, LIABILITIES AND OBLIGATIONS

**1. a.** The transfer of all powers and responsibilities to the Palestinian Authority, as detailed in Annex II, includes all related rights, liabilities and obligations arising with regard to acts or omissions which occurred prior to the transfer. Israel will cease to bear any financial responsibility regarding such acts or omissions and the Palestinian Authority will bear all financial responsibility for these and for its own functioning.

**b.** Any financial claim made in this regard against Israel will be referred to the Palestinian Authority.

**c.** Israel shall provide the Palestinian Authority with the information it has regarding pending and anticipated claims brought before any court or tribunal against Israel in this regard.

**d.** Where legal proceedings are brought in respect of such a claim, Israel will notify the Palestinian Authority and enable it to participate in defending the claim and raise any arguments on its behalf.

**e.** In the event that an award is made against Israel by any court or tribunal in respect of such a claim, the Palestinian Authority shall reimburse Israel the full amount of the award.

**f.** Without prejudice to the above, where a court or tribunal hearing such a claim finds that liability rests solely with an employee or agent who acted beyond the scope of the powers assigned to him or her, unlawfully or with willful malfeasance, the Palestinian Authority shall not bear financial responsibility.

**2.** The transfer of authority in itself shall not affect rights, liabilities and obligations of any person or legal entity, in existence at the date of signing of this Agreement.

## Article XXIII
FINAL CLAUSES

**1.** This Agreement shall enter into force on the date of its signing.

**2.** The arrangements established by the Agreement shall remain in force until and to the extent superseded by the Interim Agreement referred to in the Declaration of Principles or any other agreement between the Parties.

**3.** The five-year interim period referred to in the Declaration of Principles commences on the date of the signing of this Agreement.

**4.** The Parties agree that, as long as this Agreement is in force, the security fence erected by Israel around the Gaza Strip shall remain in place and that the line demarcated by the fence, as shown on attached map No. 1, shall be authoritative only for the purpose of this Agreement.

**5.** Nothing in this Agreement shall prejudice or preempt the outcome of the negotiations on the interim agreement or on the permanent status to be conducted pursuant to the Declaration of Principles. Neither Party shall be deemed, by virtue of having entered into this Agreement, to have renounced or waived any of its existing rights, claims or positions.

**6.** The two Parties view the West Bank and the Gaza Strip as a single territorial unit, the integrity of which will be preserved during the interim period.

**7.** The Gaza Strip and the Jericho Area shall continue to be an integral part of the West Bank and the Gaza Strip, and their status shall not be changed for the period of this Agreement. Nothing in this Agreement shall be considered to change this status.

**8.** The Preamble to this Agreement, and all Annexes, Appendices and maps attached hereto, shall constitute an integral part hereof.

Done in Cairo this fourth day of May, 1994.

FOR THE GOVERNMENT OF             FOR THE P.L.O.
THE STATE OF ISRAEL

WITNESSED BY:

THE UNITED STATES OF AMERICA             THE RUSSIAN FEDERATION

THE ARAB REPUBLIC OF EGYPT

# NOTES

## 1. My Identity as a Christian Palestinian

1. Othmar Keel and Max Küchler, *Orte und Landschaften der Bibel,* vol. 2, *Der Süden* (Göttingen: Vandenhoeck & Ruprecht, 1982), 627.

2. Tuma Bannura, *Bethlehem, Beit Sahour, Beit Jala "Ephrata"* (Jerusalem, 1982), 138.

3. For detailed information see D. J. Chitty, *The Desert a City* (Oxford: Blackwell, 1966).

4. For more on the establishment of these churches, see Friedhelm Winkelman, *Die östlichen Kirchen in der Epoche der christologischen Auseinandersetzungen* (Kirchengeschichte in Einzeldarstellungen I/6, ed. Gert Händle et al.; Berlin, 1983).

5. For more about these churches, see Donald Attwater, *The Uniate Churches of the East* (London: Geoffrey Chapman, 1961); and Joseph Hajjar, *Les Chretiens Uniates du Proche Orient* (Paris: Edition du Seuil, 1962).

6. For more about these churches, see Raymond Etteldorf, *The Catholic Church in the Middle East* (New York: Macmillan, 1959).

7. For the history of the founding of these two churches, see M. Raheb, *Das Reformatorische Erbe unter den Palästinensern: zur Entstehung der Evangelish-Lutherishen Kirche in Jordanien* (Gütersloh: Gütersloher Verlagshaus, 1990).

8. The Presbyterian Church did not play as important a role in Palestine as it did in Egypt, Lebanon, and Syria. For more on the history, see Peter Kawerau, *Amerika und die orientalischen Kirchen: Ursprung und Anfang der amerikanischen Mission unter den Nationalkirchen Westasiens* (Arbeiten zur Kirchengeschichte 31; Berlin: 1959).

9. Helmut Class, ed., *Christen im Mittleren Osten: Eine Informationsbroschüre der Evangelischen Mittelost-Kommission* (Frankfurt/Main), 44.

10. Ibid., 43–44.

11. For more information on Schneller, see Raheb, *Das Reformatorische Erbe,* 62–64.

12. For more on this parish, see ibid., 79–81.

13. Ibid., 213–15.

14. Wolfgang Hage, "Die kirchliche Situation in der vorislamischen Zeit," *Kirche im Raum des Islam,* ed. Willi Hoepfner (Christentum und Islam, 1; Breklum: 1971), 9ff.

15. Wolfgang Hage, "Der Einfluss des orientalischen Christentums auf den werdenden Islam," *Der Islam als nachchristliche Religion,* ed. Willi Hoepfner (Breklum: 1971), 7ff.

16. Wolfgang Hage, "Die kirchliche Situation," 21.

17. Bannura, *Bethlehem,* 35.

18. Ibid., 36.

19. Ibid., 139.

20. We have to estimate the number of Christians in the Middle East, because there are no official statistics available.

21. Robert Haddad, *Syrian Christians in Muslim Society: An Interpretation* (Princeton: 1970).

22. Norman Daniel, *The Arabs and Medieval Europe* (New York: Longman, 1983).

23. Albert Hourani, *Arabic Thought in the Liberal Age, 1789–1939* (Cambridge: 1983).

24. Keel and Küchler, *Orte und Landschaften,* 606ff.

25. For more on the etymology of this word, see ibid., 613.

26. Yehuda Karmon, *Israel, eine geographische Landeskunde* (Wissenschaftliche Länderkunde, ed. Werner Storkebaum, 22; Darmstadt: 1983).

27. George Antonios, *The Story of the Arab National Movement* (New York: Capricorn Books, New York: 1965).

28. Michael Krupp, *Zionismus und Staat Israel: Ein geschichtlicher Abriss* (Gütersloh: 1983).

29. These promises are known as the McMahon-Husain Correspondence, the Sykes-Picot Promise, and the Balfour Declaration. These documents are contained in Laqueur, W., ed., *Der Weg zum Staat Israel: Die Geschichte der Zionismus* (Vienna: 1975), 9–36.

30. For detailed information, see Alexander Flores, "Die Entwicklung der palästinensische Nationalbewegung bis 1939," in *Die Palästina-Frage 1917–1948:*

*Historische Ursprünge und internationale Dimensionen eines Nationalkonfliktes,* Helmut Mejcher and Alexander Schölch eds. (Sammlung Schöningh zu Geschichte und Gegenwart; Paderborn: 1981), 89–118.

31. The Palestine question was debated in the United Nations in 1947 at the request of the British government. The United Nations adopted a resolution on November 29, 1947, to end the British Mandate in Palestine, and proposed the division of Palestine into two states: a Jewish State that was supposed to take over 56 percent of Palestine's territory, and an Arab State that was supposed to have 42 percent of Palestine; Jerusalem and its surrounding area, about 2 percent of the territory, was to become an international area. The Arab majority, comprising about two-thirds of the population at that time, could not accept this proposed division, and uprisings took place all over Palestine. Zionist commandos attacked many Palestinian villages and Palestinian sections of towns. British troops left Palestine on May 15, 1948, one day before the State of Israel was proclaimed. Arab forces marched into Palestine, and the Jewish-Arab war started. By the end of the fighting in April 1949, the State of Israel occupied a larger area than the United Nations had proposed in its 1947 resolution. Egypt and Jordan divided the Arab portion of Palestine. Egypt took the Gaza Strip and Jordan the West Bank.

32. John Bunzl, *Israel und die Palästinenser: Die Entwicklung eines Gegensatzes* (Vienna: 1982), 68. For detailed information see Christoph Ülinger, *Palestinian Localities Destroyed after 1948: A Documentary List,* 2 (St. Sulpice: Association pour reconstruire Emmaeus, 1989).

33. For the results of research concerning the deportation and refugee status of the Palestinians, see Bunzl, *Israel und die Palästinenser,* 49–59.

34. Abdallah Frangi, PLO und Palästina: Vergangenheit und Gegenwart (Frankfurt: 1982).

35. Ali H. Qleibo, *Before the Mountains Disappear: An Ethnographic Chronicle of the Modern Palestinians* (A Klorens Book; Cairo: 1992), 83.

36. Ibid., 82.

## 2. On Being a Minority

1. Kemal Karpat, "The Ottoman Emigration to America, 1860–1914," *International Journal for Middle Eastern Studies* 17 (1985), 175–209.

2. Robert Brenton Betts, *Christians in the Arab East: A Political Study* (Athens: 1975), pp. 66–69.

3. Adnan Mussalam, "The Formative Stages of Immigration to the Americas until the Eve of 1948 Catastrophe," *Al-Liqa* 2 (December 1992), 26–30.

4. Betts, *Christians in the Arab East*, 67–69.

5. Ibid., 69–70.

6. M. Hassassian, "The Economic and Political Motive for Palestinian Arab Immigration since the Year of Catastrophe 1948," *Al-Liqa* 2 ( December 1992), 62.

7. Ibid, 65. See also Jack Joseph Beltritti, "The Problem of Christian Emigration from Jerusalem and the West Bank since the War of June 1967" (Jerusalem: unpublished, 1970).

8. B. Sabella, "Christian Immigration: A Comparison of the Jerusalem, Ramallah and Bethlehem Area," *Al-Liqa* 2 (December 1992), 123–43.

9. For more information, see George Kossaifi, "Demographic Characteristics of the Arab Palestinian Population," Khalil Nakleh and Elia Zureik, eds., *The Sociology of the Palestinians*, (London: Croom Helm, 1980).

10. Betts, *Christians in the Arab East*, 71–77; see also Daphne Tsimhoni, "Demographic Trends of the Christian Population in Jerusalem and the West Bank 1948–1978," *The Middle East Journal* 37 (1983), 43–64.

11. Ibid., 62.

12. Petra Held, "Christen im Nahost-Konflikt," *Deutsches Pfarrerblatt* 12 (1989) 482–85.

# 3. The Cry for Justice

1. K. Koch, "Gemeinschaftstreu/heilvoll sein," Ernst Jenni, ed., *Theologisches Handwörterbuch zum Alten Testament* vol. 2 (Munich: Chr. Kaiser Verlag, 1976), col. 514.

2. The word *Intifada* means "shaking off." It is the Palestinian attempt to get rid of the Israeli occupation. For more about the Intifada, see Alexander Flores, *Intifada: Aufstand der Palästinenser* (Berlin: 1988); and Friedrich Schreiber, *Aufstand der Palästinenser: Intifada, Fakten und Hintergründe* (Opladen: 1990).

3. Schreiber, *Aufstand der Palästinenser*, 14ff.

4. For more information on the Camp David Agreement, see Reiner Bernstein, "Das Abkommen von Camp David—Geschichte und Folgen," in *Der Frieden und die Palästinenser—Drei Jahre nach Camp David* (Berlin: Info-Service des Deutsch-Israelischen Arbeitskreises für Frieden im Nahen Osten e.V., 1982).

5. This resolution was adopted by the U.N. Security Council after the Six Day War on October 2, 1967; it states:

The Security Council . . . Emphasizing the inadmissibility of the acquisition of territory by war and the need to work for a just and lasting peace in which every state in the area can live in security:

1. Affirms that the fulfillment of Charter principles requires the establishment of a just and lasting peace in the Middle East which should include the application of both the following principles:

i) Withdrawal of Israel's armed forces from territories occupied in the recent conflict.

ii) Termination of all claims or states of belligerency and respect for the acknowledgement of the sovereignty, territorial integrity and apolitical independence of every State in the area and their right to live in peace within secure and recognized boundaries free from threats and acts of force.

2. Affirms further the necessity:

a) of guaranteeing freedom of navigation through international waterways in the area;

b) of achieving a just settlement of the refugee problem;

c) of guaranteeing the territorial inviolability and political independence of every State in the area, through measures including the establishment of demilitarized zones. . . .

6. This resolution was adopted by the Security Council on October 22, 1973, after the October War; it reaffirms Resolution 242, calling for its immediate implementation.

7. It is worth noting that the well-known Zionist slogan, "A land without people for a people without land" was introduced by a (Fundamentalist) Christian. The seventh Earl of Shaftesbury wrote in his diary on May 15, 1854: "The Turkish Empire is in rapid decay; every nation is restless; all hearts expect some great thing. . . . No one can say that we are anticipating prophecy; the requirements of it seem nearly fulfilled: Syria 'is wasted without an inhabitant'; these vast and fertile regions will soon be without a ruler, without a known and acknowledged power to claim domination. The territory must be assigned to some one or other; can it be given to any European potentate? To any American colony? to any Asiatic sovereign or tribe? Are there aspirants from Africa to fasten a demand on the soil from Hamath to the river of Egypt? No, no, no! There is a country without a nation; and a nation without a country. His own once loved, nay, still loved people, the sons of Abraham, of Isaac, and of Jacob." See Edwin Hodder, *The Life and Work of the Seventh Earl of Shaftesbury* (K.G.), 14.

8. Friedrich Schreiber and Michael Wolfssohn, *Nahost: Geschichte und Struktur des Konflikts* (Augsburg, 1987), 283ff.

9. Flores, *Intifada*, 35.

10. David Kahan, *Agriculture and Water Resources in the Westbank and Gaza (1967–1978)* (Jerusalem: 1987).

11. Simcha Bahiri, *Industrialization in the West Bank and Gaza* (Jerusalem: 1987).

12. For extensive information on social welfare, see Meron Benvenisti, *The Westbank Handbook: A Political Lexicon* (Jerusalem: 1986); and Sara Roy, *The Handbook: A Political Lexicon* (Jerusalem: 1986).

13. For more about the law, see Bunz, *Der Nahostkonflikt,* 210ff.

14. Flores, *Intifada,* 31ff.

15. Ibid.

# 4. Arab Christians in the Near East

1. For information concerning non-Muslims in the Islamic Empire, see A. Fattal, *Le Status Legal des Non-Musulmans* (Pages d'Islam; Beirut: 1958).

2. N. Fisher, *The Middle East: A History* (London: 1971), 216.

3. See M. Raheb, *Das reformatorische Erbe unter den Palästinensern* (Gütersloh, 1990), 28–30.

4. D. Tsimhoni, *The British Mandate and the Arab Christians in Palestine, 1920–1925* (London: 1976), 109.

5. N. Fisher, *The Middle East,* 213.

6. For more information on this point, see M. Maoz, *Ottoman Reform in Syria and Palestine 1840–1861: The Impact of the Tanzimat on Politics and Society* (London: 1968).

7. Quoted by A. R. Sinno, *Deutsche Interessen in Syrien und Palästina, 1840–1898: Aktivitäten religiöser Institutionen, wirtschaftliche und politische Einflüsse* (Studium zum modernen islamischen Orient, III; Berlin: 1982), 11.

8. For more on this topic, see A. Hourani, *Arabic Thought in the Liberal Age, 1798–1939* (Cambridge: 1983).

9. Ibid., 245.

10. Ibid., 255.

11. Ibid., 252.

12. Ibid., 258.

13. M. Shafiq, *al-Fikr al-Islami al-mu'aser at-tahadiyat, al-nasher* (Beirut: 1991), 27–40.

14. A. Hourani, *Arabic Thought,* 317–23.

15. M. Shafiq, *al-Fikr al-Islami,* 27–40.

16. For more about Qutb, see Adnan Musallam, "On the Road to the Gallows: Sayyid Qutb's Career and Thought, 1952–1966," *Bethlehem University Journal* (August 1985): 32–61. See also Yvonne Yazbeck Haddad, "Sayyid Qutb: Ideologue of Islamic Revival," in *Voices of a Resurgent Islam,* ed. John Esposito (New York: 1983).

17. See Z. Abu Umru, *Al Harakah al Islamiyah fi ad Difah al Garbiyah wa Qita'* (Gaza: Akko, 1989), 28–42.

18. K. Schneider (ed.), *Staat und Religion in Israel* (Berlin:1984), 75–104; and Ian Lustick, *Jewish Fundamentalism in Israel: For the Land and the Lord* (New York: 1988).

19. Z. Abu Umru, *Al Harskah*, 29–30.

20. "Das Kairos-Dokument: Ein theologischer Kommentar zur politischen Krise in Südafrika" (*Epd Dokumentation* 21/86; 1985), 28–40. The English text can be found in *Kairos: Three Prophetic Challenges to the Church,* ed. R. McAfee Brown (Grand Rapids: Eerdmans, 1990), 15–66.

21. Dietrich Bonhoeffer, *Widerstand und Ergebung: Briefe und Aufzeichnungen aus der Haft,* ed. E. Bethge (Gütersloh:1983), 155.

22. Ibid.

23. Ibid., 178.

24. Ibid.

25. *Die Zeit ist das Schlussdokument und andere Texte* (Geneva: Weltversammlung für Gerechtigkeit, Frieden und Bewahrung der Schöpfung, 1990), 18.

26. Ibid., 17.

## 6. A Personal Perspective

1. Citation from Martin Luther's introduction to the first Wittenberg edition of his writings in 1539. Karen Bornkamm and G. Ebeling, *Martin Luther: Ausgewählte Schriften* vol.1 (2d ed.; Frankfurt: Insel Verlag, 1983), 23.

2. See Eva Fleischner, ed., *Auschwitz: Beginning of a New Era? Reflections on the Holocaust* (New York, 1977).

3. See, for example, "Christen und Juden II: Zur theologischen Neuorientierung im Verhältnis zum Judentum," *Eine Studie der EKD* (Gütersloh, 1991), 21ff.

4. Ibid., 30ff.

5. Marc H. Ellis and Rosemary Radford Ruether, eds., *Toward a Jewish Theology of Liberation* (Maryknoll, N.Y. : Orbis Books, 1987).

6. See Raheb, *Das Reformatorische Erbe,* 170–85.

7. See Ateek, *Justice,* 77ff.

8. See D. Nestle, *Neues Testament Elementar* (Neukirchen: Vluyn, 1980), 51ff.

9. Klaus Koch, article "Sdq: Gemeinschaftstreu/heilvoll sein," in Ernst Jenni, *Theologisches Handwörterbuch zum Alten Testament,* vol. 2 (Munich, 1976), col. 514.

10. G. Liedke, *Gestalt und Bezeichnung alttestamenticher Rechtssätze. Eine formgeschichtlich-terminologische Studie,* (Neukirchen: Vluyn, 1971), 73.

# 7. Election

1. See Werner H. Schmidt, *Alttestamentlicher Glaube in seiner Geschichte* (4th ed.; Neukirchen: Vluyn, 1984), 117ff.

2. The New Revised Version has *known,* but as the issue is one of election, the translator chose to use the term used by the author, *chosen.*

3. Kurt Stürmer, "Auferstehung und Erwählung," *BFChTh.M* 53 (1953), 161.

4. The literature on Romans 9–11 is voluminous. See, for example, Ernst Käsemann "An die Römer," *HNT* 8 (Tübingen: 1974); H. Schlier, "Der Römerbrief," *HThKNT* VI (Freiburg, Basel, Wien: 1977); U. Wilkens, "Der Brief an die Römer, Römer 6–11," EKK VI/2 (Zürich, Einsiedeln, Köln, Neukirchen: Vluyn, 1980); and U. Luz, *Das Geschichtsverständnis des Paulus* (München: 1986).

5. Nikolaus Walter, "Zur Interpretation von Römer 9–11," *ZThK* 81 (1984), 172–95.

6. C. H. Ratschow, "Die Religionen," *HSysTh,* 16 (1979), 126.

7. Shemaryahu Talmon, "Partikularismus und Universalismus aus jüdischer Sicht," *FrRu* 28 (1976), 35.

# 8. The Promise of Land

1. See Walter Kickel, *Das gelobte Land: Die religiöse Bedeutung des Staates Israel in jüdischer und christlicher Sicht* (Munich: Kösel, 1984), 64–66.

2. Hans Küng, *Das Judentum* (Munich: Piper, 1991), 675–78.

3. Norbert Lohfink, quoted from page 5 of a transcript of a debate held in the Dormition Abbey on Mount Zion on March 1, 1992.

4. The January 11, 1980, resolution of the Landessynode der Evangelischen Kirche im Rheinland, regarding the renewal of relationships between Christians and Jews.

5. Küng, *Das Judentum,* 675–78.

6. Ibid.

## 9. The Exodus

1. *Gemeindebrief der Evangelischen Erlöser Gemeinde Jerusalem,* (May/June 1990), 15–16.

2. Ibid.

## Conclusion

1. Werner Monselewski, Der barmherzige Samariter. *Eine auslegungsgeschichtliche Untersuchung zu Lukas 10:25–37* (Tübingen: Paul Siebeck, 1967), 18–20.

# BIBLIOGRAPHY

Aburish, Said K. *The Forgotten Faithful: The Christians of the Holy Land.* London: Quartet Books, 1993.

*al-Mausu'a al Falstiniya* [The Encyclopedia of Palestine]. Four volumes. Damascus, 1984–.

Anschütz, H., and P. Harb. *Christen im Vorderen Orient: Kirchen, Ursprünge, Verbreitung, Dokumentation.* Aktueller Informationsdienst moderner Orient, Sondernummer 10. Hamburg, 1985.

Arberry, Arthus J., editor. *Religion in the Middle East.* Two volumes. Ann Arbor: Books on Demand, 1969.

Arens, Edmund. "Der schwierige Weg zur Solidarität: Theologische Beiträge zum Nahostkonflikt." In *Orientierung* 3 (1990): 29–32.

Ateek, Naim Stephan, and Rosemary Radford Ruether, editors. *Faith and the Intifada: Palestinian Christian Voices.* Maryknoll, N.Y.: Orbis, 1991.

———. *Justice, and Only Justice: A Palestinian Theology of Liberation.* Maryknoll, N.Y.: Orbis, 1989.

Betts, Robert B. *Christians in the Arab East.* Revised edition. Atlanta: John Knox Press, 1978.

Bushell, G. *Churches of the Holy Land.* New York: 1969.

Carmel, Alex. *Christen als Pioniere im Heiligen Land: Ein Beitrag zur Geschichte der Pilgermission und des Wiederaufbaus Palästinas im 19. Jahrhundert.* Basel: 1981.

Chakmakjian, Hagop A. *In Quest of Justice and Peace in the Middle East: The Palestinian Conflict in Biblical Perspective.* New York: Vantage, 1980.

Charcour, Elias, and Mary E. Jensen. *We Belong to the Land.* San Francisco: Harper, 1990.

Class, Helmut, editor. *Christen im Mittleren Osten: Eine Informationsbroschüre der Evangelischen Mittelost-Kommission.* Frankfurt/Main, n.d.

Colby, Saul P. *Christianity in the Holy Land: Past and Present.* Tel Aviv: Arn Hasefer, 1969.

Cragg, Kenneth. *The Arab Christian: A History in the Middle East.* Westminster: John Knox Press, 1991.

Damm, Thomas. *Palästinensische Befreiungstheologie: Annäherung und Würdigung aus der Sicht eines deutschen Theologen.* Kulturverein Aphorism A, Heft 5. Trier: 1992.

Davies, W. D. *The Gospel and the Land.* Berkeley: University of California Press, 1974.

——. *The Territorial Dimension of Judaism: With a Symposium and Further Reflections.* Minneapolis: Fortress Press, 1991.

Dick, Ignace. *As Sarq al-Masihi.* Min Turahtina, volume 1. Beirut: 1975.

Ellis, Marc. *Toward a Jewish Theology of Liberation: The Uprising and the Future.* 2d edition. Maryknoll, N.Y.: 1989 [1987].

——. "Critical Thought and Messianic Trust: Reflections on a Jewish Theology of Liberation." In *The Future of Liberation Theology: Essays in Honor of G. Gutiérrez.* Marc H. Ellis and Otto Mandura, editors; Maryknoll, N.Y.: Orbis, 1989. 375ff.

——. *Über den jüdisch-christlichen Dialog hinaus: Solidarität mit dem palästinensischen Volk.* Volume 1. Trier: 1992.

Fishman, Hertzel. *American Protestantism and a Jewish State.* Detroit: Wayne State University Press, 1973.

Graf, Georg. *Geschichte der christlichen Arabischen Literatur.* Studi et Testi, 4 vols. Rome: 1944–53.

Haddad, Robert. *Syrian Christians in a Muslim Society: An Interpretation.* Princeton: 1970.

Hadawi, Sami. *Christianity at the Crossroads.* Ottawa: Jerusalem International Publishing House, 1982.

——. *The Jews, Zionism, and the Bible.* Toronto: Arab Palestine Association, 1981.

Hartmann, Klaus-Peter. *Untersuchungen zur Sozialgeographie christlicher Minderheiten im Vorderen Orient.* Beihefte zum Tübinger Atlas des Vorderen Orient, Reihe B, No. 43. Wiesbaden: 1980.

Heyer, Friedrich. *Kirchengeschichte des Heiligen Landes.* Stuttgart: 1984.

Horner, Norman H. "A Guide to the Churches of the Middle East." In Wilbert Shenk, et al., eds., *Present-Day Christianity in the Middle East and North Africa.* Elkhart, Ind.: Mennonite Board of Mission.

*Im Lande der Bibel: Neue Folgen der neuesten Nachrichten aus dem Morgenland.* Berlin 1: 1955–.

Jaeger, David and Maria A., editors. *Papers Read at the 1970 Tantur Conference on Christianity in the Holy Land.* Jerusalem: Franciscan Printing Press, 1981.

Kanisatuk. *Monatsschrift der Evangelisch-Lutherischen Kirche in Jordanien.* 1954–.

Khoury, Geries S. *Guide to the Church in the Holy Land.* Nazareth: 1984.

———. *The Intifada of Heaven and Earth.* Jerusalem: 1989.

———. *Theology and the Local Church in the Holy Land.* Jerusalem: 1988.

Khoury, Rafiq. *Palästinensisches Christentum: Erfahrungen und Perspektiven.* Kulturverein Aphorism A. Heft 7. Trier: 1993.

Kickel, Walter. *Das Gelobte Land: Die religiöse Bedeutung des Staates Israel in jüdischer und christlicher Sicht.* Munich: Kösel, 1984.

Küng, Hans. *Das Judentum.* Munich: Piper, 1991.

Löffler, Paul. *Arabische Christen im Nahostkonflikt.* Frankfurt/Main: 1976.

Mejcher, Helmut, and Alexander Schölch, editors. *Die Palästina-Frage 1917–1948: Historische Ursprünge und internationale Dimensionen eines Nationenkonflikts.* Sammulung Schöhningh zur Geschichte und Gegenwart. Paderborn: 1981.

Mu'assat ad-Dirasat al-Alastiniya, editor. *Christians, Zionism and Palestine: A Selection of Articles and Statements on the Religious and Political Aspects of the Palestine Problem.* Beirut: 1970.

Osterbye, P. *The Church in Israel: A Report on the Work and Position of the Christian Churches in Israel, with Special Reference to the Protestant Churches and Communities.* Lund: 1970.

Raheb, Mitri. *Das reformatorische Erbe under den Palästinensern: zur Entstehung der Evangelisch-Lutherischen Kirche in Jordanien.* Gütersloh: Gütersloher Verlagshaus, 1990.

———. "Evangelische Theologie und Palästina: Eine kritische Auseinandersetzung mit der deutschen 'Israel-Theologie.'" In *Epd Entwicklungspolitik* Band 3 (1989): 14–18.

———. "Bibelauslegung im israelisch-palästinensischen Kontext." In *Gemeindebrief der Erlöserkirche in Jerusalem* 1–11 (1991): 16–20.

———. "Die Zukunft des heiligen Landes: Wege zu einem positiven religiösen Beitrag." In *Gemeindebrief der Erlöserkirche in Jerusalem* (December 1990 and February 1991), 9–13.

Ruether, Rosemary Radford and H. J. Ruether. *The Wrath of Jonah: The Crisis of Religious Nationalism in the Israeli-Palestinian Conflict.* San Francisco: Harper, 1989.

Schoon, Simon. "Chriestlijke presentie in de Joodse Staat." In *Dissertationes Neerlandicae, Series theologica* volume 6. Kampen, 1982.

——. "Christliche Präsenz im jüdischen Staat." In Peter von der Osten-Sacken, editor, *Veröffentlichungen aus dem Institut Kirche und Judentum* Band 17. Berlin: 1986.

Sim'an, I. "De arabische Christenheid." *Nes Ammim Lezingen* (1977/78).

Schneider, U. *Land ist unser Leben: Galiläische Dörfer im Nahostkonflikt.* Soziologie und Anthropologie Bd.5. Frankfurt/Main: Bern, 1986.

*Theological Review of the Near East School of Theology.* Beirut: 1979.

Williamson, Roger, editor. *The Role of Religion in Conflict Situations: MECC Conference Papers.* Uppsala: 1991.

——, editor. *The Holy Land in the Monotheistic Faiths.* Uppsala: Life and Peace Institute, 1992.

Younan, Mounib a. "Reflexionen eines palästinensischen Pfarrers: Christliche Existenz im Dialog mit Anderen." In *Im Lande der Bibel* 1 (1992): 24–31.

# BIBLE CITATIONS AND REFERENCES

## Old Testament

## New Testament